CASUAL DAY HAS GONE TOO FAR

A DILBERT® BOOK BY SCOTT ADAMS

Andrews and McMeel
A Universal Press Syndicate Company
Kansas City

http://www.unitedmedia.com/comics/dilbert

ISBN: 0-8362-2899-5

Library of Congress Catalog Card Number: 96-79238

For

Pam "Why-Do-You-Sneeze-When-I-Talk?" Okasaki

Other DILBERT Books from Andrews and McMeel

Fugitive from the Cubicle Police
ISBN: 0-8362-2119-2

Still Pumped from Using the Mouse
ISBN: 0-8362-1026-3

It's Obvious You Won't Survive By Your Wits Alone
ISBN: 0-8362-0415-8

Bring Me the Head of Willy the Mailboy!
ISBN: 0-8362-1779-9

Shave the Whales
ISBN: 0-8362-1740-3

Dogbert's Clues for the Clueless
ISBN: 0-8362-1737-3

Build a Better Life by Stealing Office Supplies
ISBN: 0-8362-1757-8

Always Postpone Meetings with Time-Wasting Morons
ISBN: 0-8362-1758-6

For ordering information, call 1-800-642-6480.

Introduction

I was in the bookstore the other day, hiding in the back reading a new car buying guide, and suddenly I felt very ripped-off. I realized the book had no introduction!

This shortcoming was not mentioned anywhere on the cover of the book. In fact, I had almost finished getting all the information I needed before I even realized the introduction was missing. I felt violated. Used. Dirty.

I stomped over to the cash register, pausing only long enough to de-alphabetize some of the books in the kids section. (I do that because the children are our future, which can't possibly be a good thing, so I try to slow them down when I can.)

I waited patiently in line—to demonstrate that I am a reasonable man—then I demanded my money back. Predictably, the bookstore employee started spouting a bunch of "rules" they have about refunds. I discovered they are totally inflexible about the fact that the customer must buy the book before a refund can be issued. I argued that my ownership of the book was clearly established by all the yellow highlighting I had done. This logic fell on deaf ears.

I took a deep breath to gather my composure, muttered something unintelligible about "repeat business" and stormed over to the magazine section to catch up on my reading.

Frankly, I don't know how the bookstore stays in business with service like that.

But this ugly episode got me thinking about the value of book introductions. I realized that I have an obligation as an author to do more than just take your money. I also have an obligation to fill up a certain number of pages.

And speaking of obligations, there's still time to join Dogbert's New Ruling Class (DNRC) and get the free Dilbert newsletter too. As you've probably heard, when Dogbert conquers the world, the DNRC will form his elite inner circle. Everyone else, the so-called induhviduals, will be available as our domestic servants.

The Dilbert newsletter is free and it's published approximately "whenever I feel like it," which is about four times a year. There's an e-mail version and a snail mail version. The e-mail version is better.

E-mail subscription (preferred): write to scottadams@aol.com

Snail mail:

Dilbert Mailing List
c/o United Media
200 Madison Avenue
New York, NY 10016

S.Adams

http://www.unitedmedia.com/comics/dilbert

DOGBERT EXPLAINS LEADERSHIP

LEADERS START THEIR CAREERS AS MORONS.
S. Adams

THEY ARE DRAWN TO MEETINGS LIKE MOTHS TO A PORCH LIGHT.

THE SUCCESSFUL MORON WILL HAVE A VERY HIGH BLADDER-TO-BRAIN RATIO.
BRAIN
BLADDER

THEY PREVAIL IN ALL DECISIONS BECAUSE THEY ARE IMPERVIOUS TO LOGIC OR COFFEE.

LET'S DO IT MY WAY!
OKAY!

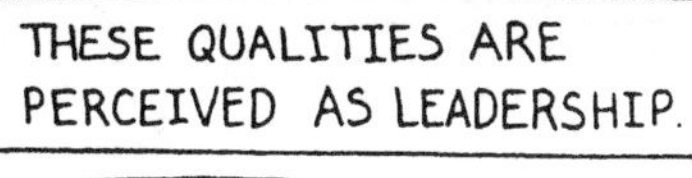
THESE QUALITIES ARE PERCEIVED AS LEADERSHIP.

YOU'RE PROMOTED!
2-5

AFTER SEVERAL PROMOTIONS THEIR JOB TENDS TO MATCH THEIR TALENTS.

I AWARD YOU THIS AWARD.

CONCLUSION: LEADERSHIP IS NATURE'S WAY OF REMOVING MORONS FROM THE PRODUCTIVE FLOW.

I'M PUTTING YOU ON THE STRATEGIC PLANNING TEAM.
S. Adams
IT'S LIKE WORK BUT WITHOUT THE SATISFACTION OF ACCOMPLISHING ANYTHING.
YOU'RE NEW, SO LET ME EXPLAIN HOW THIS WORKS.
WE HAVE MEETINGS AND TALK ABOUT THE COMPANY'S STRATEGY IN VAGUE EMOTIONAL TERMS.
IN TIME, WE CONVINCE OURSELVES THAT WE'RE MORE THAN MEDIOCRE THINKERS WHO SIT AROUND COMPLAINING.
2-12
© 1995 United Feature Syndicate, Inc.
WE START BELIEVING OUR OPINIONS WILL STEER THE COMPANY. WE FEEL IMPORTANT. WE FEEL ALIVE!!
THEN WE SNAP OUT OF IT AND MAKE VIEWGRAPHS THAT SAY WE SHOULD KEEP DOING WHAT WE'RE DOING.
I LIKE MAKING VIEW-GRAPHS.
ACTUALLY, WE USE LAST YEAR'S VIEWGRAPH.

I'M ASKING EVERYBODY TO QUANTIFY THEIR CONTRIBUTIONS TO REVENUE. YOUR PAY WILL DEPEND ON IT.
2/13
S. Adams

I REALIZE THIS IS HARD TO QUANTIFY BECAUSE YOU'RE DESIGNING FUTURE PRODUCTS BUT...
HERE YOU GO.

A BILLION DOLLARS? IT'S AS IF YOU CYNICALLY BELIEVE WE CAN'T TRACK THESE NUMBERS.
THAT CROSSED MY MIND.

YOU SHOULD ALL FOLLOW WALLY'S EXAMPLE OF HOW HE QUANTIFIES HIS CONTRIBUTION TO REVENUE.
S. Adams

BASICALLY, I ASSUMED MY PROJECT WOULD FAIL WITHOUT ME. THEREFORE ALL THE REVENUE IT GENERATES CAN BE ATTRIBUTED TO ME.

AREN'T WE ALL ON THE SAME PROJECT?
YES, BUT EVIDENTLY WE'RE NOT ALL EQUALLY VALUABLE.

WALLY, YOU JUST SENT ME THE SAME E-MAIL YOU SENT LAST WEEK.
S. Adams

I'M RERUNNING THE "BEST OF WALLY" WHILE I'M ON IN-CUBE SABBATICAL.

HOW LONG IS YOUR SABBATICAL?
SIX MONTHS SO FAR, AND YOU'RE THE FIRST TO NOTICE.

I WAS SO LATE I HAD TO PUT ON MY MAKEUP IN THE CAR.
YEAH, I HAD TO SHAVE IN THE CAR.
S. Adams
2/16

THAT'S NOTHING. I WAS SO LATE THAT I HAD TO GIVE MYSELF A SPONGE BATH IN THE CAR.

AREN'T YOU THE DRIVER FOR YOUR CARPOOL?
YOU'VE NEVER HEARD SUCH WHINING.

THE PROBLEM...
WE'RE SO UNDER-STAFFED THAT THE PROJECT IS SIX WEEKS BEHIND SCHEDULE.
S. Adams

THE ANALYSIS...
I CAN'T ADD PEOPLE... I CAN'T CHANGE THE DUE DATE... I CAN'T IGNORE IT.
2/17

THE RESULT...
HE WANTS DAILY STATUS REPORTS UNTIL THE SITUATION IMPROVES.

BAD NEWS
WE'RE NOT GIVING ANY RAISES.
S. Adams

MAKING IT WORSE
BUT WE THINK WORK IS ITS OWN REWARD.

MAKING IT MUCH WORSE
EXPECT TO GET REWARDED ABOUT TWICE AS MUCH NEXT YEAR.

BOSS TYPES
FIND YOUR BOSS ON THIS HANDY REFERENCE.
S. Adams

HOSTAGE TAKER: TRAPS YOU IN YOUR CUBICLE AND TALKS YOUR EARS OFF.
BLAH BLAH
OW!!

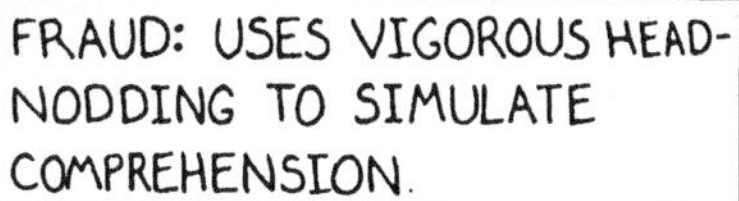
FRAUD: USES VIGOROUS HEAD-NODDING TO SIMULATE COMPREHENSION.

THEN WE'LL SUBNET OUR I.P. ADDRESSES.
OH YEAH OH YEAH

MOTIVATIONAL LIAR: HAS NO CLUE WHAT YOU DO BUT SAYS YOU'RE THE BEST.
NOBODY CAN DO WHAT YOU DO!!
EXCEPT A MUSHROOM.

OVER PROMOTED: TRIES TO MASK INCOMPETENCE WITH POOR COMMUNICATION.
LET'S QUALITIZE OUR PARADIGM SO WE DON'T OVER INUNDATE WITH DATUMS.

WEASEL: TAKES CREDIT FOR YOUR HARD WORK.
THIS BONUS IS FOR BRILLIANTLY FORCING YOUR STAFF TO WORK 80 HOUR WEEKS.
IT WASN'T EASY!
$
2-19

MOSES: PERPETUALLY WAITS FOR CLEAR SIGNALS FROM ABOVE.
DON'T DO ANYTHING IMPORTANT YET.
NEVER HAVE.

PERFECT BOSS: DIES OF NATURAL CAUSES ON A THURSDAY AFTERNOON.
SHOULD WE DO SOMETHING?
THREE DAY WEEKEND!

RELIABLE SOURCES SAY YOUR PROJECT WILL BE CANCELLED, DILBERT.
2/20

YOU SHOULD ABANDON IT NOW AND COME WORK ON MY PROJECT. WHEN MY BIG PROMOTION GOES THROUGH NEXT MONTH, I'LL TRANSFER YOU TO MY GROUP AND GIVE YOU A RAISE.
S. Adams

THAT'S VERY TEMPTING EXCEPT FOR THE FACT YOU'RE A PATHOLOGICAL LIAR.
BE CAREFUL WHAT YOU SAY - I HAVE SUPER POWERS.
© 1995 United Feature Syndicate, Inc.

DOGBERT, I NEED YOUR HELP DEALING WITH A PATHOLOGICAL LIAR AT WORK.
2/21

YOU'RE IN LUCK. I HAPPEN TO HAVE A PH.D. IN LIATOLOGY FROM THE MASSACHUSETTS INSTITUTE OF TECHNOLOGY.
S. Adams

I'D LOVE TO SEE YOUR DIPLOMA.
I'LL MAIL IT TO YOU.
© 1995 United Feature Syndicate, Inc. (NYC)

WE'VE BEEN HAVING A PROBLEM WITH BLACK-OUTS. THE OFFICE LIGHTS ARE CONTROLLED BY MOTION DETECTORS.
S. Adams

I HIRED A TEMP TO WALK AROUND AND FLAP HIS ARMS SO THE LIGHTS WON'T GO OFF.
2/22 © 1995 United Feature Syndicate, Inc. (NYC)

ANOTHER JOURNALISM MAJOR ENTERS THE WORKFORCE.
IT SEEMS LIKE A WASTE. MAYBE HE COULD FAN US.

ALICE, I'M ALMOST DONE WITH YOUR PERFORMANCE APPRAISAL.
GASP
S. Adams

I HAVEN'T HAD AN APPRAISAL IN FOUR YEARS. YOU MUST BE STARTING A DOCUMENTATION TRAIL SO YOU CAN FIRE ME LATER.
2/23
© 1995 United Feature Syndicate, Inc. (NYC)

I'LL WORK 24 HOURS A DAY!!
THAT WAS WAY MORE MOTIVATIONAL THAN I'D HOPED.

I'M TERRIFIED ABOUT MY PERFORMANCE REVIEW TOMORROW.
2/24
S. Adams

MEN HAVE IT EASIER. YOU'VE BEEN CONDITIONED BY YEARS OF REJECTION AND GENERAL DISDAIN.
WE'RE LUCKY THAT WAY.
© 1995 United Feature Syndicate, Inc. (NYC)

OVERALL, I RATED YOUR PERFORMANCE AS "SIMIAN."
THANKS!

I'VE REPLACED THE OLD RATING SYSTEM WITH A FRIENDLIER METHOD. NOW I COMPARE EACH OF YOU TO AN ANIMAL WITH SIMILAR TRAITS.
S. Adams

I RATED YOU "TYRANNOSAURUS REX."
2/25
© 1995 United Feature Syndicate, Inc. (NYC)

T. REX – THE MIGHTIEST DINOSAUR!!
THINK IN TERMS OF BRAIN SIZE.

HERE'S SOME NICE CHOCOLATE CAKE FOR YOU AND DOGBERT.
THANKS, MOM.
THANKS, MOM.
S. Adams
TELL ME ALL ABOUT YOUR JOB AT THE RAILROAD.
IT'S NOT A RAILROAD. I'M AN ENGINEER AT A BIG CORPORATION.
DO YOU FIX THE TYPEWRITERS WHEN THEY BREAK?
NO... TODAY I DEBUGGED A TCP/IP DRIVER FOR AN APPLICATION THAT RUNS OVER ISDN WITH BONDING.
© 1995 United Feature Syndicate, Inc.
YOU MEAN, ALL YOU DO IS SLAP A BRI ANALYZER ON A CIRCUIT AND LOOK FOR BAD PACKETS?
2-26
WELL... YEAH.
BUT IT'S REALLY HARD.
I WAS DOING OKAY UNTIL SHE OFFERED TO PAY MY TUITION TO TYPEWRITER REPAIR SCHOOL.
YOU SHOULDN'T HAVE COMPARED HER CAKE TO PACKING FOAM.

I'M HAPPY TO REPORT THAT THE "EXCELLENCE IN TEAMING" READ-OUT IS NEARLY READY.

IT'S TAKEN FORTY PEOPLE FROM A DOZEN DEPARTMENTS TO COMPLETE THE STUDY. WE FINALLY GOT COMPLETE BUY-IN.

IS THAT THE STUDY OF WHY WE CAN'T MAKE DECISIONS?
ORIGINALLY. BUT IT EVOLVED INTO MORE OF A DISCUSSION OF SQUIRREL MIGRATION PATTERNS.
2/27

AND TED GETS THIS "SINGULAR ACHIEVEMENT" AWARD FOR CREATING THE "WE ARE TEAMS" CAMPAIGN.

IT'S A CHECK FOR A THOUSAND DOLLARS! LET'S ALL GIVE TED A HAND.

SLAP
WHACK
OW!!
THESE THINGS NEVER WORK THE WAY YOU WANT THEM TO.
2/28

WHY IS IT THAT I NEVER HAVE TIME TO EAT BUT YOU MEN ARE IN HERE EVERY DAY AT 11:35?
3/1

BECAUSE THE HOURS WE SPENT UPGRADING OUR PCs HAVE FINALLY PAID OFF BY GREATLY IMPROVING OUR EFFICIENCY.

I THOUGHT IT WAS BECAUSE WE GET HUNGRY AT 11:30.
WE CAN'T REVEAL ALL OUR SECRETS.

WE'RE ANNOUNCING TWO NEW PROGRAMS FOR EMPLOYEES.
S. Adams

THE FIRST IS A NEW DIGNITY ENHANCEMENT PROGRAM AND THE SECOND IS OUR NEW RANDOM DRUG TESTING INITIATIVE.

THE CLUE METER IS READING ZERO.
YOU EACH GET A HANDSOME COFFEE MUG AS PART OF THE KICK-OFF.

DROP YOUR TROUSERS AND TURN AROUND. I NEED A DNA SAMPLE.
3/3

S. Adams
WE'RE SCANNING FOR ANY FATAL GENETIC PROBLEMS THAT COULD HURT PRODUCTIVITY.

UH... WE DECIDED TO MOVE YOUR PROJECT DEADLINE UP A WEEK.

FROM NOW ON, SALARIES WILL BE BASED ON YOUR PREDICTED SUCCESS, NOT YOUR PAST PERFORMANCE.
3/4

S. Adams
WE RAN A COMPUTER MODEL AGAINST YOUR EDUCATION AND DNA INFORMATION. WE PREDICT YOU'LL DIE IN A STAPLER MISHAP WITHIN A WEEK.

WHAT IF I DISAGREE WITH THIS PREDICTION?
WRITE UP YOUR OPINION AND STAPLE IT TO THE ANALYSIS.

WE'RE GOING DOWNTOWN TO PLAY "SECURITY GUARDS IN SPACE."
I DON'T WANT TO KNOW.
GEEK WEEK
S. Adams
LET'S TRY THAT BUILDING.
LUNCH
I'LL NEED TO SEE YOUR I.D. BADGE, SIR.
LOOK FAST!! THERE IT IS!! NOT A PACK OF MATCHES!!
OKAY
ZIP!
I'LL HAVE TO SEARCH YOUR LUNCH BOX.
© 1995 United Feature Syndicate, Inc.
IT'S JUST A BUNCH OF WIRES AND GIZMOS.
YOU'RE MAKING ME SO HUNGRY.
LUNCH
COULD YOU WATCH MY LUNCH WHILE I TAKE THE CART BACK TO MY CAR?
3-5
I FEEL BAD, BUT IT'S THE ONLY WAY TO TEST IF SPACE TRAVEL IS SAFE FOR US ANIMALS.
I FEEL SAFER ALREADY.

CAN YOU EXPLAIN WHY YOU'RE A WEEK BEHIND SCHEDULE?
S. Adams

YOUR POOR LEADERSHIP HAS DRAINED ME OF THE ENTHUSIASM THAT IS NECESSARY TO SUCCEED. BUT IT'S NOT COMPLETELY YOUR FAULT.
3-6

FRANKLY, YOUR PARENTS HAVE TO ACCEPT SOME RESPONSIBILITY FOR CREATING YOU.
EVEN IF THEY WERE DRUNK?

WE NEED TO FINISH YOUR PROGRAM TWICE AS FAST, SO I'M ADDING A PERSON TO HELP YOU.
S. Adams

YOU MIGHT NEED TO TRAIN HIM A LITTLE BEFORE HE'S PRODUCTIVE.
WARNING! WARNING! DR. SMITH

TELL ME AGAIN WHAT THE BIG GLOWING THING IS.

ARE YOU WORKING TWICE AS FAST SINCE I DOUBLED YOUR STAFF?
S. Adams

I'VE CODED TWELVE MODULES... BARRY IS ON A JOURNEY OF DISCOVERY WHERE HE WILL FIND OUT MY MOUSE IS NOT A MICROPHONE.
HELLO! ANYBODY!

THAT WOULD EXPLAIN WHY NOBODY EVER COMMENTS ON MY ANNOUNCEMENTS OVER THE P.A. SYSTEM.

FROM NOW ON, THE MANAGERS AT MY LEVEL WILL BE CALLED "THOUGHT LEADERS."
S. Adams

WHAT'S WRONG WITH THIS PICTURE?

YOUR PERFORMANCE THIS YEAR WAS GOOD, BUT YOU WORKED ON TASKS THAT AREN'T IMPORTANT. THEREFORE YOU GET A TINY RAISE.
S. Adams

I WORKED ON THE TASKS YOU ASSIGNED. WHAT'S THAT SAY ABOUT YOUR PERFORMANCE?

IT'S EXCELLENT. I GET A BONUS FOR KEEPING SALARIES LOW.
HAVE YOU SEEN ANY LITERATURE ON WORKPLACE VIOLENCE?

UH-OH... THE MANAGERS ARE GOING TO ANOTHER CLOSED-DOOR MEETING.
S. Adams

IT MUST BE ABOUT PAY CUTS OR LAYOFFS. I'M DOOMED. I'D BETTER WORK ON MY RÉSUMÉ NOW.

OKAY, SO FAR OUR "LEADERSHIP VISION" SAYS "WE INSPIRE EMPLOYEES TO ACTION." DOES ANYBODY HAVE UPGRADES?
NAH

DID YOU REVIEW MY DRAFT DOCUMENTATION YET?
UH... I'LL GET TO IT SOON.
S. Adams

THAT'S WHAT YOU'VE BEEN SAYING SINCE JULY!!

I KNOW I'M ONLY A LOWLY TECHNICAL WRITER AND YOU'RE A BIG IMPORTANT ENGINEER...

BUT IS IT TOO MUCH TO ASK FOR YOU TO GLANCE AT THE FRUITS OF MY LABORS?!!!

FIVE LOUSY MINUTES IS ALL IT WOULD TAKE TO VALIDATE MY VALUE ON THIS PLANET! READ IT, YOU FETID PILE OF COMPOST!!
© 1995 United Feature Syndicate, Inc.

OKAY, OKAY! I'LL READ IT RIGHT NOW!

THESE PAGES ARE BLANK! YOU'VE BEEN BLUFFING FOR MONTHS!
3-12

I THINK I'LL GO HAVE A YUMMY COMPOST SALAD WITH DELICIOUS FETID CHEESE.
I'M GOING TO LOOK UP THOSE WORDS.

I PROMISE THAT IF I DECIDE TO BUY YOUR COMPANY I'LL GLADLY RECOMMEND A POSITION FOR EACH OF YOU.

S. Adams
REALLY? YOU'D MAKE SURE WE ALL GOT JOBS?
3-13 © 1995 United Feature Syndicate, Inc. (NYC)

NO, BUT I'LL RECOMMEND A "POSITION."

MY CONSULTANT WILL AUDIT YOUR COMPANY TO MAKE SURE THERE ARE NO SURPRISES BEFORE I BUY IT.

S. Adams
I USE HIM BECAUSE HE'S SEEN SUCH HIDEOUS THINGS THAT NOTHING SCARES HIM.
ERK
3-14 © 1995 United Feature Syndicate, Inc. (NYC)

AAAAAEEII!!
OOOUWAA WAA!!
THAT'S NOT THE SOUND YOU WANT FROM YOUR AUDITOR.

YOUR STOCK WAS $30 PER SHARE WHEN I OFFERED TO BUY THE COMPANY, BUT THANKS TO SOME TIMELY LEAKS TO THE MEDIA YOUR VALUE HAS PLUNGED.

S. Adams
HOWEVER, IF YOU SELL RIGHT NOW I'LL PAY THE FULL $30 FOR YOUR STOCK.
I RECOMMEND WE DO IT.
3-15 © 1995 United Feature Syndicate, Inc. (NYC)

DONE. $30 PER SHARE IS MORE THAN FAIR.
YEAH, "PER SHARE" WOULD HAVE BEEN FAIR.
ANYBODY WANT A COPY?

AS NEW OWNER OF THIS COMPANY I HEREBY BAN ALL MEETINGS OVER ONE HOUR. THE DRESS CODE IS CASUAL. STATUS REPORTS ARE OPTIONAL!
S. Adams

NO MORE MISSION STATEMENTS OR "VISIONS." OUR MOTTO IS "HAVE FUN, SATISFY CUSTOMERS, MAKE MONEY."

AND STOCK OPTIONS FOR ALL.
ZZZ
WE CAN FIT FIVE MORE IN THIS CUBICLE IF WE REMOVE THE CHAIR.

THE RUMORS ARE DESTROYING OUR PRODUCTIVITY. WE CAN'T WORK WITH ALL THIS UNCERTAINTY.
S. Adams

I PLAN TO BUY PROVEN TECHNOLOGY AND HIRE CONTRACT EMPLOYEES. YOU'LL BE GOPHERS FOR THE CONTRACTORS UNTIL YOU RESIGN IN DISGUST AND HUMILIATION.

IS THERE ANY WAY TO GET BACK TO UNCERTAINTY?
I'LL SEE WHAT I CAN DO.

NOW THAT YOU OWN THE COMPANY, WHAT DO YOU PLAN TO DO?
TRIM MIDDLE MANAGEMENT.
S. Adams

I'LL FIRE ANYBODY WHO GIVES ME A DOCUMENT MARKED "FYI." THOSE PEOPLE HAVE TOO MUCH TIME ON THEIR HANDS.

ARE YOU SURE THIS WILL SET ME APART FROM THE OTHER MANAGERS?
YOU'LL BE SURPRISED HOW QUICKLY.
FYI
FYI
FYI

SO... OKAY, GREAT...
ALRIGHT THEN...
S. Adams
I'M TRAPPED IN THE MEETING THAT WOULD NOT CONCLUDE!!
I'M TOO POLITE TO SAY "WE'RE DONE. PLEASE LEAVE."
LIKE I SAID BEFORE...
OH NO! I MISSED THE WINDOW - HE'S REITERATING!!!
SO...OKAY, GREAT...
ALRIGHT THEN...
3-19
© 1995 United Feature Syndicate, Inc.
MAYBE IF I SHAKE HIS HAND HE'LL LEAVE.
BUT LIKE I SAID BEFORE...
NOOOO OOOO!!
...THEN THERE WAS SORT OF A LONG AWKWARD PAUSE...
SO... OKAY, GREAT...

I HIRED A NEW DIRECTOR OF HUMAN RESOURCES TO HANDLE THE DOWN-SIZING.
S. Adams

I NEEDED SOMEBODY WHO ACTS LIKE A FRIEND BUT SECRETLY DELIGHTS IN THE MISERY OF ALL PEOPLE.
3-20

WE NEED TO TALK, PAUL. BUT FIRST I'M GOING TO BAT YOUR HEAD AROUND AND SCRATCH YOU.
HEE HEE!! THAT'S SO CUTE!

CATBERT THE HR DIRECTOR
HERE'S THE NEW ORG CHART. MAYBE YOU'RE ON IT AND MAYBE NOT.
S. Adams

OOH! NICE TRY! SO CLOSE. TOO BAD.
3-21

IT'S FUN TO PLAY WITH THEM BEFORE DOWNSIZING THEM.

COME SEE THE NEW ORG CHART.
S. Adams

OOPS, CHANGED MY MIND!
WHAM!!
3-22

OUCHIE.
I'M SORE, BUT I'VE NEVER FELT SO FREE.

I'VE DECIDED TO SELL THE COMPANY FOR A HUGE PROFIT. I FOUND SOME VERY DISCRIMINATING BUYERS.
S. Adams

WHEN YOU SAY DISCRIMINATING, YOU MEAN...?
THEY HATE PEOPLE FROM THIS COUNTRY.

IT'S OKAY. WE HAVE LAWS TO PROTECT US.
THEY'RE LAZY, BUT AT LEAST THEY'RE FUNNY!
HEE HEE

HOW COULD THE ELBONIANS AFFORD TO BUY THIS COMPANY? THEIR WHOLE COUNTRY IS JUST MUD.
S. Adams

THEY PACKAGED THE MUD AND SOLD IT AS A COSMETIC ON THE "COUCH SHOPPING NETWORK." THEY MADE TRILLIONS.
$119.95

AT LEAST THEY KNOW HOW TO MANAGE RESOURCES.
THEY SOLD THEIR ENTIRE COUNTRY IN LITTLE JARS. MOST ELBONIANS PERISHED IN MOLTEN LAVA AT THE EARTH'S CORE.

... BUT BY FAR, THIS COMPUTER IS OUR MOST USER-FRIENDLY.
S. Adams

THE PRE-INSTALLED SOFTWARE HAS ONLY ONE BUTTON. AND WE PRESS IT BEFORE IT LEAVES THE FACTORY.

WHAT DOES IT DO?
WHOA! I'M IN OVER MY HEAD. LET ME GIVE YOU THEIR TECH SUPPORT NUMBER.

PLEASE ENTER PHOTOCOPIER ACCESS CODE.
S. Adams
WHAT'S THE CODE FOR THIS MACHINE?
THAT'S PROPRIETARY INFORMATION.
WE WORK FOR THE SAME COMPANY. MY CUBICLE IS DOWN THE HALL.
I HAVE NO WAY OF VERIFYING YOUR CLAIM. ANY-BODY COULD COME IN HERE AND SAY THAT.
ASK ME A QUESTION THAT ONLY AN EMPLOYEE OF THIS COMPANY COULD ANSWER.
OKAY.
© 1995 United Feature Syndicate, Inc.
WHAT IS THE ACCESS CODE FOR THIS COPIER?
3-26
SOB
I JUST HAVE ONE...

IN A WAY, I'M GLAD THE ELBONIANS RUN THIS COMPANY NOW.
S. Adams

AFTER YEARS OF BEING THE ONLY FEMALE ENGINEER I'LL ENJOY WATCHING THE ELBONIANS DISCRIMINATE AGAINST YOU GUYS.

CONTINUED...
I DIDN'T REALIZE YOU HAD COFFEE WENCHES IN THIS COUNTRY TOO.
I HOPE YOU DON'T WANT CHILDREN, YORGI.

IN THIS COUNTRY WE HAVE A CUSTOM WHEN MEN ASK WOMEN TO FETCH COFFEE.
S. Adams

STAND UP... THAT'S IT... NOW THIS WILL REALLY SURPRISE YOU.
OH GOD

I'VE NEVER SEEN ANYBODY GET KICKED INTO HIS HAT BEFORE.
THAT'S GOTTA HURT.

OUR ELBONIAN OWNERS SOLD THE COMPANY TO OUR BIGGEST COMPETITOR.
S. Adams

OUR MOTTO IS "IF YOU CAN'T BEAT 'EM, JOIN 'EM."
I WONDER WHAT THEIR MOTTO IS.

THEIR MOTTO IS "AFTER YOU BEAT 'EM, HUMILIATE 'EM."
IT'S NOT VERY CATCHY.

YOU LEFT THAT ERROR IN THERE INTENTION-ALLY.

MY LAST BATCH OF FLOWERS IS WILTING.

I'D LIKE YOU GUYS TO CHECK ANNE'S ADVERTISING MATERIALS FOR TECHNICAL ACCURACY.
S. Adams

IS THIS SUPPOSED TO BE FUNNY?
I DON'T GET IT.

I'M ONLY LOOKING FOR TECHNICAL HELP HERE.

HEY! MAYBE YOU COULD SAY SOMETHING ABOUT THOSE WARNING TAGS ON MATTRESSES! NOW THAT WOULD BE FUNNY!

OR HOW ABOUT THE FACT THAT YOU CAN'T LOOK UP SOMETHING IN THE DICTIONARY IF YOU CAN'T SPELL IT? THAT'S FUNNY!

4-2

YOU'RE ENGINEERS, NOT COMEDIANS!! I WANT TECHNICAL HELP!!!

THIS GUY HAS AN XP-6. IT SHOULD BE AN XP-7.
THAT'S BETTER.

AND HE SHOULD BE SAYING "I'VE FALLEN AND I CAN'T GET UP."
WHO PICKED THESE COLORS?

MY LAPTOP COMPUTER IS LOCKED UP. CAN YOU HELP?
S. Adams

REMEMBER YOU HAVE TO HOLD IT UPSIDE DOWN AND SHAKE IT TO REBOOT.
OH, THAT'S RIGHT.

I WONDER IF HE'LL EVER REALIZE WE GAVE HIM AN "ETCH-A-SKETCH."

DOGBERT THE CONSULTANT
YOUR BEST BET IS TO RELOCATE THE COMPANY TO RUSSIA.
S. Adams

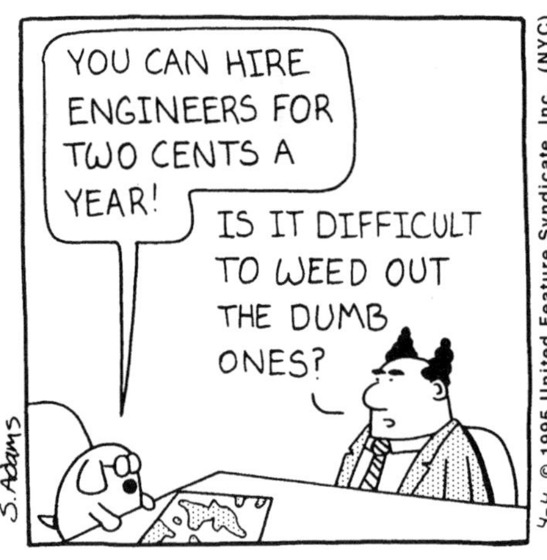
YOU CAN HIRE ENGINEERS FOR TWO CENTS A YEAR!
IS IT DIFFICULT TO WEED OUT THE DUMB ONES?

NO. AND THAT LEADS ME INTO THE GOOD NEWS ABOUT THEIR OCCUPATIONAL SAFETY LAWS.
IT'S LIKE HEAVEN!

I WANT TO ASSURE YOU THAT ANY RUMORS YOU'VE HEARD ARE FALSE.
S. Adams

WE ARE NOT PLANNING TO RELOCATE THE COMPANY TO THE SOUTH POLE WHERE EASILY TRAINABLE NATIVE ESKIMOS WILL REPLACE YOU.

THAT'S GOOD BECAUSE THERE AREN'T ANY ESKIMOS AT THE SOUTH POLE.
EXCUSE ME, I HAVE TO MAKE A PHONE CALL.
4-5

WE'RE OFFERING ATTRACTIVE INCENTIVES TO COMPANIES THAT MOVE TO ELBONIA.
S. Adams

ZERO TAXES, CHEERFUL SLAVE LABOR, AMNESTY FROM ANY INCONVENIENT LAWS, AND ABSOLUTELY NO ENVIRONMENTAL REGULATIONS!

IS THAT THE BEST YOU CAN DO?
HERE, USE MY FIRSTBORN SON AS A LAWN ORNAMENT.

TRY THIS LITTLE TRICK TO IMPROVE YOUR CAREER...
S. Adams

ANYTIME YOU WANT SOMETHING YOUR WAY, SIMPLY REFER TO YOUR CEO BY HIS FIRST NAME AND SAY HE GAVE YOU DIRECTIONS DURING YOUR VERY RECENT MEETING.

IT'S TOTALLY UNVERIFIABLE. PEOPLE WILL FEAR YOU AND DO AS YOU SAY. YOU'LL RULE WITH AN IRON FIST!
YOU'RE A FUNNY LITTLE DOG.

JUST AS I THOUGHT, MY CUBICLE IS TWO INCHES SMALLER TODAY THAN YESTERDAY!
S. Adams

WE INSTALLED REAL-TIME STATUS ADJUSTERS IN THE CUBICLE WALLS. SENSORS MONITOR YOUR WORK AND ADJUST THE CUBICLE SIZE ACCORDING TO YOUR VALUE.

IT'S AMAZING HOW FAST YOU GET USED TO IT.

WE RANKED ALL THE ENGINEERS FROM BEST TO WORST.
WE PLAN TO GET RID OF THE BOTTOM 10%. THAT INCLUDES YOU, WALLY.
S. Adams
YOUR PLAN IS LOGICALLY FLAWED.
IF YOU FIRE THE BOTTOM 10%, YOU'LL STILL HAVE A BOTTOM 10%.
YOU'LL FIRE AND FIRE BUT THERE WILL ALWAYS BE A BOTTOM 10%, UNTIL FINALLY...
© 1995 United Feature Syndicate, Inc.
WHEN LESS THAN TEN PEOPLE ARE LEFT YOU'LL HAVE TO FIRE BODY PARTS INSTEAD OF WHOLE PEOPLE!!!
WE'LL HAVE TORSOS AND GLANDS WANDERING AROUND UNABLE TO USE KEYBOARDS... BLOOD AND BILE EVERYWHERE!!!
4-9
HOW'D IT GO?
HE FIRED MY HAIR.

THIS ERGONOMIC KEYBOARD IS OUR FIRST PRODUCT DEVELOPED UNDER THE "BIG Q" PROGRAM.
S. Adams

THE "Q" STANDS FOR QUALITY.
SPEAKING OF Q... IT'S MISSING THE LETTER Q.
4-10 © 1995 United Feature Syndicate, Inc. (NYC)

YOU SOUND JUST LIKE OUR WHINY CUSTOMERS.
I GUESS THE "Q" STANDS FOR "UALITY."

OKAY, SO WE SHIPPED A MILLION KEYBOARDS THAT DON'T HAVE THE LETTER "Q." WHAT DO WE DO?
S. Adams

WE COULD OFFER FREE UPGRADES TO USERS WHO CAN PROVE THEY NEED A "Q."
4-11 © 1995 United Feature Syndicate, Inc. (NYC)

HOW MANY USERS NEED A "Q"?
WELL... THERE'S THE ROYAL FAMILY...

THE PUNDITS IN THE PRESS ARE NAILING US FOR SHIPPING A KEYBOARD WITH NO "Q."
NEWS
S. Adams

IT'S A PUBLIC-RELATIONS FIASCO. OBVIOUSLY, WE NEED AN ENGINEERING SOLUTION.
I'M ON THE CASE.
NEWS
4-12 © 1995 United Feature Syndicate, Inc. (NYC)

USERS COULD USE A GRAPHICS PROGRAM TO DRAW A "Q" IN THE UNLIKELY EVENT THAT THEY NEED ONE.
OR WE COULD REPLACE THE SEMI-COLON; NOBODY USES THEM.

YOU COULD OFFER FREE REPLACEMENTS FOR ALL THE KEYBOARDS YOU SOLD WITHOUT A "Q," OR YOU COULD BLAME THE MEDIA FOR BLOWING IT OUT OF PROPORTION.
S. Adams

LET'S BLAME THE MEDIA. THEY'LL ADMIT THEY WERE WRONG AND THE WHOLE THING WILL DISAPPEAR.

YOU HAVE A BRILLIANT GRASP OF HUMAN NATURE, WALLY.
I KNOW. MY THIRD WIFE ALWAYS SAID THE SAME THING.

DOGBERT THE PR CONSULTANT
YOU SHIPPED KEYBOARDS WITH NO LETTER "Q." THE PUBLIC WANTS SOMEBODY TO TAKE RESPONSIBILITY.
S. Adams

OOH OOH PICK ME PICK ME!!

RESPONSIBILITY MEANS BLAME.
GREAT... IT'S LIKE THE TIME I GOT BURNED ON THAT "OPPORTUNITY" ASSIGNMENT.

STICK TO THE SCRIPT. ACT SINCERE AND BEG YOUR CUSTOMERS TO FORGIVE YOU.
S. Adams

IT WAS WRONG FOR US TO SELL KEYBOARDS WITH NO "Q." WE'RE SORRY. WE'RE MORONS.

WE'RE DUMBER THAN SQUIRRELS. WE HEAR VOICES AND DO WHAT THEY COMMAND. I HAVE BROCCOLI IN MY SOCKS.
GOOD WRITING
THANKS

LOOKS LIKE SOMEBODY HAS A JOB INTERVIEW.
SHHH
S. Adams

YOUR RÉSUMÉ IS IMPRESSIVE. I ONLY HAVE ONE QUESTION.

WHAT DO YOU CONSIDER YOUR BIGGEST FAULT?

SOMETIMES I WORK TOO HARD.
GOOD ONE

WHY IS THAT A FAULT?
© 1995 United Feature Syndicate, Inc

WELL... UH... I WORK SO HARD THAT I FORGET TO EAT AND BATHE FOR DAYS. EVENTUALLY I STARVE TO DEATH AT MY DESK.
4-16

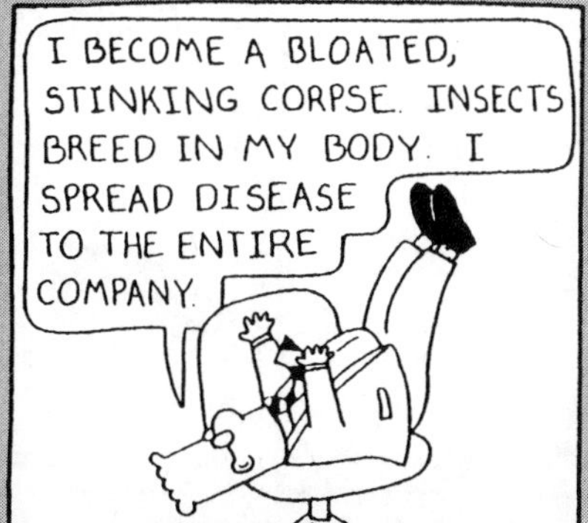
I BECOME A BLOATED, STINKING CORPSE. INSECTS BREED IN MY BODY. I SPREAD DISEASE TO THE ENTIRE COMPANY.

HOW DID IT GO?
THEY WANT SOMEBODY HUNGRIER.

I'M GOING INTO BUSINESS AS A FINANCIAL ADVISOR.
SOUNDS HARD.
S. Adams

IT'S EASY. I'LL TELL ALL MY CLIENTS TO INVEST IN THE "DOGBERT DEFERRED EARNINGS FUND."

ISN'T THAT A CONFLICT OF INTEREST?
ONLY IF I SHOW INTEREST IN THE CLIENT.

IT'S ALL TOO CONFUSING FOR YOU!! GIVE ME ALL YOUR MONEY NOW OR YOU'LL DIE A PAUPER!! NOW! NOW! BEFORE INTEREST RATES FALL!!

WILL THIS REDUCE MY INCOME TAXES?
MORE THAN YOU MIGHT GUESS.

DOGBERT: FINANCIAL ADVISOR
STOCKS... ANNUITIES... DERIVATIVES... CAPITAL GAINS TAX...
HERE'S A PICTURE OF YOU LIVING IN A DUMPSTER IN TWENTY YEARS.
S. Adams

BUT IF YOU INVEST IN THE "DOGBERT DEFERRED INCOME FUND" TAKE A LOOK AT WHAT YOU COULD OWN SOMEDAY!!

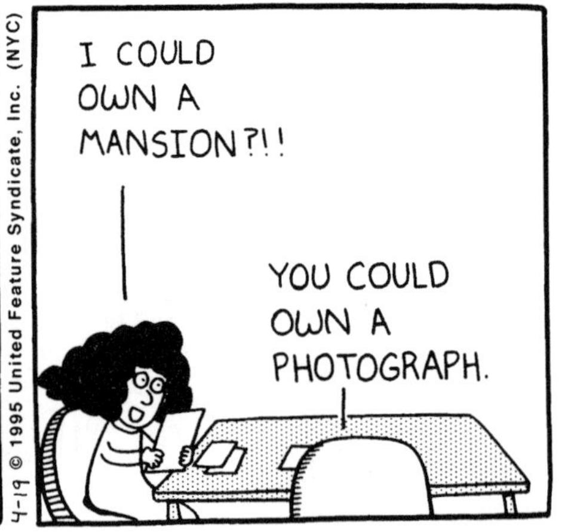

I COULD OWN A MANSION?!!
YOU COULD OWN A PHOTOGRAPH.

WE'RE MOVING TO A NEW OFFICE ACROSS TOWN. I VOLUNTEERED TO COORDINATE THE MOVE.

I CONTROL YOUR CUBICLE ASSIGNMENT. NAY, YOUR VERY EXISTENCE. FROM NOW ON YOU WILL REFER TO ME AS "LORD WALLY THE PUPPET MASTER."

S. Adams

I DON'T THINK IT'S LEGAL TO ENJOY YOUR WORK THIS MUCH.

I BANISH YOU TO THE CUBICLE CLOSEST TO YOUR BOSS!!

ALLOW ME TO INTRO-DUCE LOUD HOWARD.

S. Adams

I WILL MAKE LOUD HOWARD YOUR CUBICLE NEIGHBOR IN THE NEW OFFICE UNLESS YOU GIVE ME YOUR IMMORTAL SOUL!!

NICE DAY!

...FORTUNATELY I CONVINCED HIM TO TAKE MY LASER PRINTER INSTEAD...
WHAT DID I SAY THAT SOUNDED LIKE "TELL ME ABOUT YOUR DAY"?

"TO HEAR YOUR URGENT VOICE MAIL MESSAGE PRESS ONE..."

S. Adams

"THIS URGENT MESSAGE IS TO ALL EMPLOYEES. PLEASE DISREGARD THE RUMORS OF A MERGER WITH A HEALTHY COMPANY."

NOW SPOOKED, THE HERD STAMPEDES.
RÉSUMÉ!
WHERE'S MY INTERVIEW SUIT??!!

YOU'LL BE PERFORMING A "TURING TEST" ON OUR NEW ARTIFICIAL INTELLIGENCE SOFTWARE.
S. Adams

TRY TO DETERMINE IF THE RESPONSES ON YOUR SCREEN COME FROM OUR COMPUTER OR A HUMAN IN THE NEXT ROOM.

I'LL ASK IT TO WRITE A STRATEGY FOR OUR COMPANY.

"OUR STRATEGY IS TO VISIONIZE QUALITY RESOURCES THAT ENHANCE EARNINGS."
HMM

I'LL ASK IT HOW TO MOTIVATE EMPLOYEES.
© 1995 United Feature Syndicate, Inc.
4-23

"REORGANIZE OFTEN TO IMPROVE FOCUS. REDEFINE WORK AS 'OPPORTUNITY' AND INCREASE IT DAILY. TAKE TIME TO ASK FOR OPINIONS THEN EXPLAIN WHY THEY'RE WRONG."

IT MUST BE A COMPUTER BECAUSE THERE'S NO HUMAN INTELLIGENCE.
UNLESS...

NICE TRY, BOSS.

WE'VE GOT A LOT OF EMPTY CUBICLES BECAUSE OF DOWNSIZING.
S. ADAMS

I HIRED THE DOGBERT CONSTRUCTION COMPANY TO CONVERT PART OF THE OFFICE INTO PRISON CELLS
WHICH WE'LL LEASE TO THE STATE.

SOUNDS LIKE A BIG JOB.
NAH. A LITTLE PAINT, NEW CARPET AND WE'RE THERE.

I DON'T THINK IT'S FAIR TO PUT CONVICTS IN OUR SPARE CUBICLES.
S. ADAMS

DON'T BE SUCH A BIGOT. THESE PEOPLE HAVE MADE ONE LITTLE MISTAKE. OTHERWISE, THEY'RE JUST LIKE EMPLOYEES.

I THINK THERE ARE A FEW DIFFERENCES!
YEAH, THEIR HEALTH PLAN IS BETTER.

HEY, BUDDY, WHAT ARE YOU IN FOR?
S. ADAMS

UNLIKE YOURSELF, I AM NOT A PRISONER HERE. I CHOOSE TO WORK HERE OF MY OWN FREE WILL!

GREAT... I'M IN THE FREAK SECTION.
I LIKE TO WORK.

EFFECTIVE IMMEDIATELY, WE WILL NO LONGER USE OUR SPARE CUBICLES TO HOUSE CONVICTS.

YES!!! OUR OPINIONS MATTERED!
ACTUALLY, IT'S BECAUSE THE PRISONERS COMPLAINED.
S. Adams

I WONDER WHAT HE PLANS TO DO WITH THE SPARE CUBICLES NOW.

BAD NEWS IN 1985
WE'RE REPLACING THE COMPANY DOCTOR WITH A REGISTERED NURSE.

BAD NEWS IN 1990
WE FIRED THE NURSE AND PUT THE ASPIRIN AND TOURNIQUETS IN THE VENDING MACHINE.
S. Adams

BAD NEWS IN 1995
WE'VE BEEN ASKED TO INCREASE VENDING MACHINE REVENUE BY FIFTEEN PERCENT.

I'M PLANNING TO TURN THE HOUSE INTO A GAMBLING CASINO.

ISN'T THAT ILLEGAL?
NOT IN THE TINY REPUBLIC OF DOGBERTLAND. I SECEDED FROM THE REPRESSIVE HOMELAND THIS MORNING.
S. Adams

I DON'T REMEMBER VOTING ON THAT.
HERE'S YOUR GREEN CARD.

LET ME INTRODUCE YOU TO ONE OF OUR ENGINEERS.
S. Adams
KAREN IS OUR NEW VICE PRESIDENT. AND YOU ARE...?
DILBERT: VALUED EMPLOYEE.
I BELIEVE IN OPEN COMMUNICATIONS, DILBERT. FEEL FREE TO TALK ABOUT ANY-THING.
UH-OH
SO, WHAT WERE YOU WORKING ON?
OH-NO
WELL... I WAS JUST SENDING AN E-MAIL TO SOMEBODY WHO SITS BY A WINDOW TO ASK IF IT'S RAIN-ING.
© 1995 United Feature Syndicate, Inc.
4-30
IF IT'S RAINING I'LL FASHION A RAINCOAT FROM A LARGE TRASH BAG.
WATCH.
THREE HOLES AND YOU'RE READY TO GO!
ARE YOU PLANNING TO GO OUT AT LUNCH?
ONLY IF IT RAINS.

I THINK THE BEST WAY TO PURSUE MY GOAL OF WORLD DOMINATION IS TO BECOME A TALK RADIO HOST.
S. Adams

I'LL PROMOTE MY UNIQUE CONSERVATIVE VIEW-POINT THAT PEOPLE ARE IDIOTS WHO DESERVE TO BE MOCKED.

WON'T PEOPLE SHOW YOUR VIEWPOINT TO BE FLAWED BY VIRTUE OF THEIR INTELLIGENT QUESTIONS?
LIKE THAT ONE?

DOGBERT'S TALK RADIO
I'M THE SMARTEST CREATURE IN THE UNIVERSE AND YOU ARE ALL DOLTS.
S. Adams

TODAY I'M TAKING CALLS FROM PEOPLE WHO THINK THEY UNDERSTAND COMPLEX ISSUES BECAUSE THEY WATCH "CROSSFIRE" ON CNN.

"... SO WHY NOT PUT ALL POOR PEOPLE IN ORPHANAGES?"
PUT YOUR HEAD UP TO THE SPEAKER, BOB.

TODAY WE'RE TALKING ABOUT SEX AFTER MARRIAGE. MANY LIBERALS SUPPORT THIS DEPRAVED PRACTICE BUT I DO NOT.
S. Adams

IT CAN LEAD TO HEAD-ACHES, FATIGUE AND UNWANTED FAMILY MEMBERS WHO BECOME CONSULTANTS.

"WOULDN'T YOUR PHILOSOPHY LEAD TO THE EXTINCTION OF MANKIND?"
CRY ME A RIVER, LIBERAL.

WELCOME TO THE DOGBERT SHOW. TODAY I TALK ABOUT GETTING GOVERNMENT OFF OUR BACKS.
S. Adams

I DREAM OF A WORLD WHERE SOMEDAY YOU CAN BUY LIQUOR, CIGARETTES AND FIREARMS AT A DRIVE-THRU WINDOW AND USE THEM ALL BEFORE YOU GET HOME.
5-4 © 1995 United Feature Syndicate, Inc. (NYC)

BASICALLY, ANYTHING THAT GETS RID OF PEOPLE IS OKAY WITH ME. BUT BEFORE YOU GO, BUY MY NEW BOOK...

MY HOBBY IS GEOGRAPHY. WOULD YOU SIGN MY BOOK TO EACH OF THE CONTINENTS BY NAME?
S. Adams

ARE YOU AWARE THAT MY BOOK RECOMMENDS A TWIRLING WEDGIE FOR PEOPLE WHO ASK FOR TOO MUCH?
5-5 © 1995 United Feature Syndicate, Inc. (NYC)

WE FIND THE LINE MOVES FASTER IF I DO THIS TO THE FIRST CUSTOMER.

I'M RETIRING FROM MY MEDIA EMPIRE AND PUTTING MY VAST WEALTH INTO REAL ESTATE.
S. Adams

MY PLAN IS TO BUY ALL THE PROPERTY ON EARTH AND EVICT EVERYBODY WHO DOESN'T AGREE TO BE MY PUPPET.
5-6 © 1995 United Feature Syndicate, Inc. (NYC)

CAN I BE KERMIT?
THAT'S A "MUPPET." IT'S ALL SPELLED OUT IN YOUR LEASE.

THE 7 HABITS OF
HIGHLY
DEFECTIVE
PEOPLE
OW!

1. IGNORE ANY SIGNS OF DISCOMFORT IN OTHERS.
BUT HEY, I'VE BEEN DOING ALL OF THE TALKING.
S. Adams

2. USE HUMOR TO BELITTLE PEOPLE IN PUBLIC.
OUR NEWEST TEAM MEMBER HAS MOVIE STAR LOOKS. SPECIFICALLY, LASSIE.

3. TREAT ALL COMPLAINTS AS THE COMPLAINER'S FAULT.
YOU DON'T MOTIVATE ME.
MAYBE YOU SHOULD SEE A THERAPIST.

4. SHOW UP LATE AND RAISE CONTROVERSIAL ISSUES.
I THINK WE SHOULD LICENSE "BARNEY" AS OUR MASCOT.

5-7

5. GIVE ADVICE ON THINGS YOU DON'T UNDERSTAND.
TRY WRITING SOME ASSEMBLY LINE CODE HERE.

6. USE COMPLIMENTS TO SHOW YOUR PREJUDICES.
OOH, NICE CRISP PHOTO-COPY, ALICE. I DON'T THINK A MAN COULD HAVE DONE IT BETTER!

7. THINK THE COMICS ARE NOT ABOUT YOU
HEE HEE! LOOK AT THE HAIR ON THAT GUY!

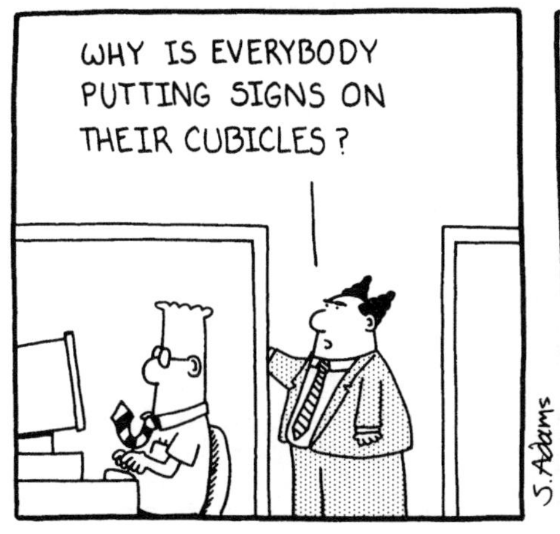
WHY IS EVERYBODY PUTTING SIGNS ON THEIR CUBICLES ?
S. Adams

WE THOUGHT IT WOULD BE CLASSY TO NAME OUR CUBICLES THE SAME WAY WE NAME CONFERENCE ROOMS.

I KNOW THERE'S A CATCH... BUT WHAT?
MENENDEZ ROOMS
O.J. ROOM

I'M SO LUCKY TO BE DATING YOU, LIZ. YOU'RE AT LEAST AN EIGHT.
YOU'RE A TEN.
S. Adams

ARE WE USING THE SAME SCALE?
TEN IS THE NUMBER OF SECONDS IT WOULD TAKE TO REPLACE YOU.

TO: ALL USERS
FROM: NETWORK ADMIN
PLEASE REFRAIN FROM FRIVOLOUS E-MAIL. IT BOGS DOWN THE NET-WORK.
S. Adams

TO: NETWORK ADMIN
FROM: DILBERT
CC: ALL USERS
I AGREE!

HAVE YOU NOTICED THERE'S TOO MUCH COMMUNICATION IN THE WORLD, DOGBERT?
YEAH, EVERY DAY AT ABOUT THIS TIME.

WE COULD SIMPLY DIVIDE THE CHECK BY THREE...
UH-OH. ENGINEERS.
S. Adams

BUT THAT WOULD RESULT IN AN UNPOPULAR SUBSIDY OF WALLY'S SALMON. DOES ANYBODY HAVE A CALCULATOR-WATCH?

THIS IS THE TIE-BREAKER ROUND OF WATER TO DECIDE IF YOU GET 13% OR 13.5%.

TODAY WE HAVE A MOTIVATIONAL SPEAKER FROM THE "DISCOUNT SPEAKERS BUREAU."

YOU SHOULD, LIKE, WORK HARDER... OTHERWISE YOU MIGHT GET FIRED. ANY QUESTIONS?

WOULD WE GET BONUSES FOR WORKING HARDER?
THIS MUST BE THE SLOW CLASS.

I'M GOING TO INTERVIEW SUCCESSFUL PEOPLE AND WRITE A BOOK OF THEIR TIPS. I'LL START WITH YOU, DOGBERT.
S. Adams

SET YOUR ALARM CLOCK TO GO OFF EVERY HOUR. KEEP A BIG VAT OF "JELL-O" BY THE BED. WHEN THE ALARM GOES OFF, STICK YOUR HEAD IN THE "JELL-O" AND YELL "BOY, I'M TIRED!"

THANKS!
BEWARE THE ADVICE OF SUCCESSFUL PEOPLE; THEY DO NOT SEEK COMPANY.

WRITE UP YOUR ACCOMPLISHMENTS SO I CAN DECIDE WHO GETS RAISES THIS YEAR.
ARE YOU SAYING OUR RAISES WILL DEPEND ON OUR ABILITY TO LIE ABOUT OUR ACHIEVEMENTS?
NO, THERE'S ALSO FAVORITISM.
AND DON'T FORGET THE IMPORTANCE OF MINIMIZING THE ACCOMPLISHMENTS OF OTHERS.
S. Adams
"THIS YEAR I SAVED A BILLION DOLLARS IN WAYS WHICH ARE IMPOSSIBLE TO VERIFY."
"WHILE THE OTHERS PLOTTED AGAINST YOU, I WAS APPLYING AN INVISIBLE RUST INHIBITOR TO YOUR CAR."
© 1995 United Feature Syndicate, Inc.
5-14
I CAN DROP THOSE OFF FOR YOU.
THANKS.
HAVE YOU NOTICED SHE'S THE ONLY ONE WHO EVER GETS A RAISE?
IT'S AS IF SHE HAS THE ACCOMPLISHMENTS OF THREE PEOPLE.

WHO NEEDS TO SIGN MY BUSINESS CASE TO BUY A WEB SERVER?

HMM... THIS CROSSES ALL DEPARTMENTS. I FEAR IT. GET THE APPROVAL OF EVERY DIRECTOR, EVERY VP, EVERY EVP, PLUS GRIFFIN.
S. Adams

DO YOU MEAN TED GRIFFIN IN FINANCE OR THE MYTHICAL GRIFFIN BEAST THAT'S HALF EAGLE, HALF LION?
WHICHEVER IS HARDER.

I COULD GIVE YOU MARKETING'S APPROVAL RIGHT NOW...
S. Adams
OR I COULD FLEX MY VICE PRESIDENTIAL POWER AND SEND YOU TO GATHER MORE USELESS DATA... MY EGO WOULD EXPAND AND I'D BE A MAJOR STALLION WITH MY WIFE TONIGHT.

DO YOU THINK YOU CAN TOP THAT?
I'LL TRY, SIR. WHAT'S YOUR WIFE'S ADDRESS?

I NEED YOUR APPROVAL ON MY BUSINESS CASE, TOM.
S. Adams

I'LL WEDGE IT IN HERE SO YOU CAN CLAIM YOU NEVER SAW IT WHEN I ASK ABOUT IT NEXT WEEK.
THANKS

THE WEIRD PART IS THAT I CAN FEEL PRODUCTIVE EVEN WHEN I'M DOOMED.

TODAY I DISTRIBUTED 36 COPIES OF MY BUSINESS CASE TO VARIOUS MANAGERS FOR APPROVAL.
S. Adams

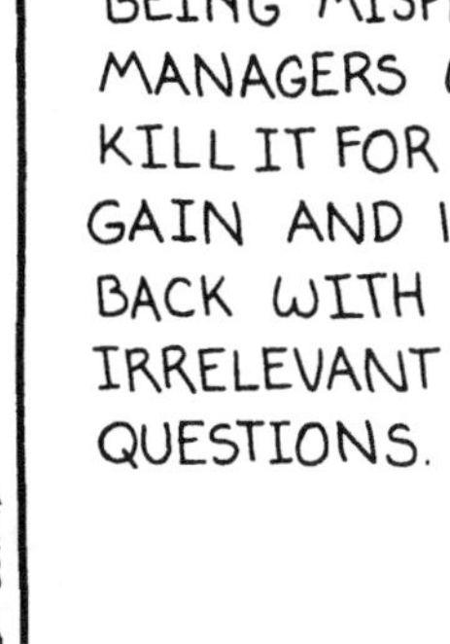
BY MY COUNT, 20 ARE BEING MISPLACED, 6 MANAGERS WILL TRY TO KILL IT FOR PERSONAL GAIN AND 10 WILL COME BACK WITH IRRELEVANT QUESTIONS.

WHEN I DIE I WANT TO BE BURIED, NOT CREMATED, SO I CAN AT LEAST MAKE ONE LASTING IMPRESSION ON THE EARTH.
I WAS PLANNING TO MAIL YOUR CORPSE TO SOMEBODY I DON'T LIKE.

WE NEED TO BOOST OUR RETURN-ON-ASSETS RATIO.
S. Adams

LET'S ELIMINATE THE SECURITY DEPARTMENT. THAT WOULD CUT EXPENSES WHILE ALLOWING FOR A BRISK REDUCTION IN ASSETS.

WHEN ARE YOU PLANNING TO TELL HIM YOU WERE JOKING?
AFTER I FURNISH MY DEN.

YOU NEVER ANSWERED MY E-MAIL.
S. Adams

MY SECRETARY IS OUT, SO THERE'S NOBODY TO PRINT MY E-MAIL FOR ME. BRING ME YOUR MESSAGE ON HARDCOPY.

I WAS OUT OF PAPYRUS SO I CHISELED MY MESSAGE ON A LITTLE PYRAMID.
DID HE WORK ALONE OR WERE UFOs INVOLVED?

HERE'S THE COMPANY VISION AND BUSINESS PLAN.
S. Adams
"VISION: EMPOWERED EMPLOYEES WORKING TOWARD A COMMON PLAN."
SOUNDS GOOD.
BUT THE BUSINESS PLAN IS BLANK.
IT'S CONFI-DENTIAL.
HOW AM I SUPPOSED TO KNOW WHAT TO DO?
I'LL YELL AT YOU IF YOU DO THE WRONG THING.
I THOUGHT I WAS EMPOWERED.
DON'T BE SO LITERAL.
© 1995 United Feature Syndicate, Inc.
5-21
I'LL JUST KEEP DOING WHAT I WAS DOING.
NO!!! YOU FOOL!!!
WE'RE DOOMED, AREN'T WE?
I DON'T KNOW. I HAVEN'T SEEN THE PLAN.

OUR POLICY IS TO EMPLOY ONLY THE BEST TECHNICAL PROFESSIONALS.
QUESTION.
S. Adams

ISN'T IT ALSO OUR POLICY TO BASE SALARIES ON THE INDUSTRY AVERAGE?

RIGHT. WE LIKE THEM BRIGHT BUT CLUELESS.
I FEEL SORRY FOR PEOPLE LIKE THAT.

MY SALARY DEPENDS ON YOUR OPINION OF MY WORK. BUT YOU HAVE NO INTEREST IN UNDERSTANDING WHAT I DO, SO...
S. Adams

I HIRED THE DOGBERT PUBLIC RELATIONS FIRM TO HYPE MY PERFORMANCE AND GET ME A BIG RAISE.

PRESS RELEASE: ENGINEER CURES CANCER WHILE SAVING BABY FROM BURNING BUILDING.
THAT'S NOT IN HIS OBJECTIVES.

YOU CAN CREATE THE ILLUSION THAT YOU WORK LONG HOURS BY LEAVING VOICE MAILS FOR YOUR BOSS AT 4A.M.
S. Adams

HI, THIS IS DILBERT. IT'S 4 A.M. AND I'M IN MY UNDERWEAR AND I THOUGHT OF YOU... OOPS... ERASE... OOPS...
BEEP BEEP

DID YOU JUST SEND AN OBSCENE MESSAGE TO YOUR BOSS?
NO... I THINK I HIT THE GROUP CODE.

TELL ME YOUR GREATEST ACCOMPLISHMENTS AT WORK. I'LL USE THAT TO HYPE YOU UP WITH YOUR BOSS SO YOU GET A BIG RAISE.
S. Adams

I WROTE A DRAFT OF A WHITE PAPER ON A STRAWMAN PROCESS TO REENGINEER OUR PRODUCT PROCESS.
5/25 © 1995 United Feature Syndicate, Inc. (NYC)

AND WHAT WAS THE IMPACT OF THAT WORK?
I THINK SOME OWLS LOST THEIR WOODLAND HABITATS.

YOU MUST LEARN TO USE YOUR BOSS'S IGNORANCE TO YOUR ADVANTAGE.
S. Adams

FIND OUT WHAT IMPRESSES HIM AND LIST IT ON YOUR ACCOMPLISHMENTS.
5/26 © 1995 United Feature Syndicate, Inc. (NYC)

YOU'RE THE ACTOR IN THE "BARNEY" SUIT?!! I LOVE THAT GUY!
DON'T TELL ANYBODY MY SECRET IDENTITY.

IN MY DREAM I FLOAT OVER FIELDS OF HEATHER.
Hi! I'M Heather
S. Adams

THE FLYING DREAM ALWAYS PREDICTS AN IMPORTANT CHANGE. I FEEL THAT MY FREE-DOM WILL SOON INCREASE.
5/27 © 1995 United Feature Syndicate, Inc. (NYC)

DOES SOMEBODY ELSE HAVE A QUESTION FOR OUR NEW CEO?
MY FINGER IS STUCK.

I'M PUTTING YOU IN CHARGE OF PROJECT "BIFF."
DILBERT
"BIFF" STANDS FOR "BIG IMPROVEMENTS FOR FREE."
YOUR JOB IS TO RECOMMEND WAYS TO INCREASE PROFITS WITHOUT SPENDING MONEY OR CHANGING ANYTHING.
YOU HAVE TO SPEND MONEY TO MAKE MONEY.
IF WE HAD MONEY TO SPEND WE WOULDN'T NEED TO MAKE MONEY.
DUH
S. Adams
THE POINT IS THAT YOU CAN MAKE MORE MONEY THAN YOU SPEND.
I'M NOT FOLLOWING YOUR SO-CALLED "POINT."
5-28
© 1995 United Feature Syndicate, Inc.
LOGICALLY, ANYTHING I DON'T UNDERSTAND IS UNIMPORTANT.
HAVE YOUR REPORT TOMORROW.
SO, YOU RECOMMEND... REPLACING ALL MANAGERS WITH LAVA LAMPS.
HERE'S A FEW BUCKS FOR THE LAVA LAMPS.

I'VE DECIDED TO BE MORE OF A HANDS-ON MANAGER.

MOVE THE MOUSE... UP... UP... OVER... MORE... **NOW CLICK IT!! CLICK IT!!**
S. Adams
5/29 © 1995 United Feature Syndicate, Inc. (NYC)

NO!!! YOU FOOL!!!
THIS HAS "LONG DAY" WRITTEN ALL OVER IT.

HAVE YOU TAKEN THE MANDATORY TRAINING FOR BUSINESS ETHICS?
S. Adams

NO. BUT IF YOU SAY I DID THEN YOU'LL SAVE SOME MONEY ON TRAINING WHICH YOU CAN SPEND TO DECORATE YOUR OFFICE.
5/30 © 1995 United Feature Syndicate, Inc. (NYC)

LUCKILY, I HAVEN'T TAKEN THE TRAINING MYSELF.
I HEAR IT'S MOSTLY COMMON SENSE ANYWAY.

HEY! THAT LITTLE STUFFED DOLL LOOKS JUST LIKE ME!
S. Adams

IT GIVES ME AN EMOTIONAL LIFT TO HAVE YOUR LIKENESS NEARBY.
5/31 © 1995 United Feature Syndicate, Inc. (NYC)

I NEVER REALIZED WHAT HE THOUGHT OF ME.
STOP DROPPING IN LIKE THAT!!
WHACK!

MY CELLULAR PHONE AND LAPTOP COMPUTER ALLOW ME TO WORK ANY TIME AND ANYPLACE...

S. Adams

WHILE DRIVING?
TOO DANGEROUS
IN RESTAURANTS?

OUTDOORS?

BASICALLY, YOU LUG THEM AROUND AND WORRY THAT THEY'LL GET STOLEN OR BROKEN.
STOP IT. YOU'RE SCARING THEM.

WHAT'S THE HAT FOR, WALLY?
IT'S A NEW SAFETY RULE. I THINK IT'S STUPID.

S. Adams

THE E-MAIL FROM HUMAN RESOURCES SAID ALL SHORT EMPLOYEES MUST WEAR THESE TO IMPROVE VISIBILITY WHILE IN THE CUBICLE AISLES.

HR SHOULD CHANGE THEIR PASSWORD ONCE IN A WHILE.
I'LL BET WE CAN MAKE HIM WEAR ALUMINUM FOIL PANTS.

HERE'S YOUR LATEST BUDGET CUTS. BUT PLEASE DON'T KILL THE MESSENGER FROM FINANCE, HA HA!!

S. Adams

I RECOMMENDED A 20% CUT. A QUICK GLANCE AROUND THE ROOM TELLS ME YOU'RE NOT ON THE SUCCESS VECTOR ANYHOO, SO NOTHING LOST.

TOUGH ROOM.

YOUR COMPANY MAKES AN ATTRACTIVE LITTLE PRODUCT, JIM.
BUT WE'VE DECIDED TO GO WITH A VENDOR WHOSE PRODUCT ACTUALLY WORKS.
S.ADAMS
FOOLS!!! I'LL CRUSH YOU!!!
I'LL TELL YOUR BOSS YOU MADE A STUPID DECISION!! YOUR CAREERS WILL BE RUINED AND I'LL GET THE CONTRACT
ANY-WAY!!
YOU CAN'T SCARE US! DO YOU THINK OUR BOSS WILL BELIEVE A VENDOR OVER HIS OWN LOYAL EMPLOYEES?
© 1995 United Feature Syndicate, Inc.
MUST... KEEP... A... STRAIGHT... FACE...
6-4
HA HA HA HA HA HA HA HA
WE'LL TAKE A MILLION UNITS.
TAKE TWO MILLION AND I'LL SEE THAT YOU GET NICE RAISES.

WHY DO YOU WANT TO TRANSFER TO MY DEPARTMENT, WALLY?
S. Adams

I'M IN A DYSFUNCTIONAL ORGANIZATION. I'M NOT GETTING THE LOVE AND SUPPORT I NEED. THAT'S WHY I'VE BEEN MAKING LONG-DISTANCE PERSONAL CALLS FROM THE FAX ROOM.

6/5

YOUR RÉSUMÉ SAYS EVERY BOSS YOU'VE HAD WAS A COMPLETE JERK.
SO, WHEN DO I START?

I HIRED RENOWNED PSYCHOLOGIST DOGBERT TO HELP US ACHIEVE PEAK PERFORMANCE IN TEAMWORK.
S. Adams

PEAK PERFORMANCE IS SOMEWHAT RELATIVE. YOU'RE A HIGHLY DYSFUNCTIONAL TEAM,
SO WE MUST SET REALISTIC GOALS.

6/6

WHAT WOULD BE A REALISTIC GOAL FOR US?
I THINK I CAN POSTPONE CANNABILISM.

DYSFUNCTIONAL TEAM...
I'D LIKE EVERYBODY TO TURN TO THE RIGHT AND SAY WHAT YOU ADMIRE ABOUT THAT PERSON.
S. Adams

I ADMIRE YOUR LEATHERY SKIN, ALICE.
I ADMIRE YOUR ABILITY TO FIGURE OUT WHICH SIDE IS YOUR RIGHT IN ONLY TWO TRIES.

6/7

I ADMIRE YOUR ABILITY TO GET PAID FOR THIS.
DESPITE THE FACT YOUR FACE SCARES CHILDREN, I ADMIRE YOUR CO-WORKERS.

IN THIS TEAM-BUILDING EXERCISE YOU WILL MAKE PAPER DOLLS WHILE BLINDFOLDED.
S. Adams

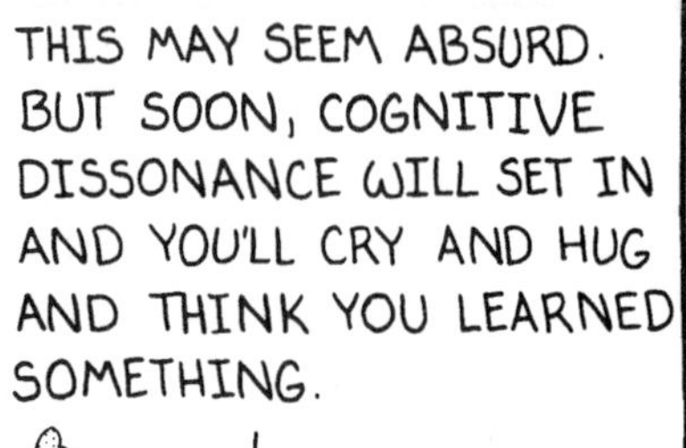
THIS MAY SEEM ABSURD. BUT SOON, COGNITIVE DISSONANCE WILL SET IN AND YOU'LL CRY AND HUG AND THINK YOU LEARNED SOMETHING.

ARE YOU SURE WE'LL CRY AND HUG?
ACTUALLY, HUGGING IS IFFY.

DYSFUNCTIONAL TEAM...
I'D LIKE EACH OF YOU TO TELL THE TEAM WHAT YOU LEARNED IN MY WORKSHOP.
S. Adams

I LEARNED TO LISTEN WITH MY HEART. I GAINED RESPECT FOR OTHERS. I UNDERSTAND SANSKRIT. I GOT MY HAM RADIO LICENSE. I CAN DIVIDE BY ZERO...

I LOVE GOING FIRST.

YOU'VE GOT TO INCREASE THE BUDGET FOR TRAINING!
S. Adams

IF I TRAIN YOU, THEN WOULDN'T YOU JUST LEAVE THE COMPANY TO MAKE MORE MONEY WORKING FOR OUR COMPETITOR?
I GUESS THERE IS A DOWN-SIDE.
AND THE DOWNSIDE WOULD BE...?

LET'S GO AROUND THE CIRCLE AND SHARE WHAT WE LEARNED IN THE THREE-DAY WORKSHOP.
TEAM
S. Adams
AT FIRST I THOUGHT IT WAS A WASTE OF OUR TRAINING BUDGET...
THEN YOU ASKED US TO FORM TEAMS AND MAKE PAPER AIRPLANES WHILE BLINDFOLDED...
I DON'T KNOW IF IT WAS BECAUSE OF THE DARKNESS OR THE WAY WE SHARED OUR THOUGHTS ABOUT FLIGHT...
BUT SUDDENLY I FOUND UNCONDITIONAL LOVE FOR MY CO-WORKERS.
BE THEY ACCOUNTANTS, BE THEY MARKETEERS OR BE THEY SECRETARIES.
© 1995 United Feature Syndicate, Inc.
6-11
AS A RESULT, I'VE BECOME A COMPETITIVE LION, EAGER TO POUNCE ON MY WORKLOAD AND INCREASE STOCKHOLDER VALUES!!
THANK YOU, WALLY.
DILBERT, WHAT DID YOU LEARN?
I LEARNED THAT YOU SHOULDN'T PUT A LITTLE ERASER-PILOT IN YOUR PAPER AIRPLANE.
SOMEBODY NEEDS A GROUP HUG!

HAVE FUN WORKING. I'M OFF TO THE TWO-WEEK MANAGEMENT RETREAT IN THE MOUNTAINS.
S. Adams

IT'S SO SAD YOU CAN'T COME. I GUESS THERE ISN'T ROOM AT THE FOUR-STAR HOTEL.

NOW I KNOW WHY IT'S CALLED A RETREAT.

HELLO, IS THIS THE MOUNTAIN RESORT WHERE ALL OUR EXECUTIVES ARE HAVING A RETREAT?
S. Adams

IS IT TRUE THAT LOUD NOISES CAN CAUSE AVALANCHES?
IF YOU SEE MY BOSS, TELL HIM I SAID...

HI!!

GREAT NEWS! I'VE REENGINEERED YOUR JOB TO MAKE YOU MORE FULFILLED!
S. Adams

YOU'LL NO LONGER BE LIMITED TO ONE LITTLE PART OF THE VALUE CHAIN. YOU'LL BE INVOLVED IN ALL STAGES OF PRODUCTION!

OH LORD, YOU FIRED ALL THE SECRETARIES!!
DUST MY CREDENZA.

LACKING CLERICAL SUPPORT, THE HIGHLY TRAINED, HIGHLY PAID PROFESSIONALS LINE UP AT THE COPIER.
S. Adams

THEIR AMAZING ANALYTICAL SKILLS ARE SQUANDERED IN THIS MINDLESS TASK.
6/15 © 1995 United Feature Syndicate, Inc. (NYC)

NO... IT LOOKS LIKE THE "TONER" LIGHT DOESN'T TURN OFF IF YOU WAIT.
LET'S GIVE IT ANOTHER FIVE MINUTES.

MY NEW GOAL, BOB, IS TO BE THE NEXT HEAVY-WEIGHT BOXING CHAMPION OF THE WORLD!!
S. Adams

DON'T LET ANYBODY EVER TELL YOU THAT YOU'RE TOO SMALL OR TOO SLOW OR TOO UNCOORDINATED.
6/16 © 1995 United Feature Syndicate, Inc. (NYC)

OR TOO CLUELESS.
EXACTLY! NOW YOU'RE CATCHING ON.

I SEE SIGNS OF PRODUCTIVITY HERE. I'M MOVING YOU TO ANOTHER CUBICLE.
DILBERT
S. Adams

YOUR PHONE AND COMPUTER WILL BE DISCONNECTED FOR WEEKS. YOUR FILES WILL BE BOXED AND LOST.
6/17 © 1995 United Feature Syndicate, Inc. (NYC)

GOOD LORD, YOU'VE ABANDONED ALL PRETENSE OF BEING ON OUR SIDE!!
LOSER

I'VE BEEN INVITED TO BE A GUEST ON "CROSSFIRE" ON CNN.
S. Adams

I'M THE ONLY CREATURE ON EARTH WHO HASN'T ALREADY BEEN ON TELEVISION.

CAN YOU TEACH ME HOW TO DEBATE ON TELEVISION, DOGBERT?
OKAY

FIRST, RATBERT, ASSUME EVERYBODY HAS THE SAME DESIRES AND EXPERIENCES AS YOU.
ABSORB ABSORB

THEREFORE, IF THEY DISAGREE WITH YOU THEY MUST BE STUPID.

6-18

I THINK YOU'RE OVER-SIMPLIFYING, DOGBERT.

WHAT WAS THAT OPINION, RATBERT?
STUPID!

YOU'RE READY FOR "CROSSFIRE," RATBERT.
I USUALLY LIKE THE SAME MOVIES AS THE FAT ONE.

I'VE BEEN HIRED BY THE FINANCE DEPARTMENT TO HELP CUT SPENDING.
S. Adams

I'LL BE STUDYING YOUR EVERY MOVE AND LOOKING FOR WASTE AND INEFFICIENCY.
6/19 © 1995 United Feature Syndicate, Inc. (NYC)

THOSE WORDS IN BOLDFACE LOOK LIKE THEY'RE SUCKING UP THE OL' ELECTRICITY.

I'M FROM THE FINANCE DEPARTMENT. I'M HERE TO REDUCE COSTS.
S. Adams

IT MIGHT SEEM LIKE ALL I DO IS COME UP WITH SHORT-SIGHTED WAYS TO SAVE MONEY WHILE MAKING YOUR JOB HARDER. BUT THERE'S ANOTHER SIDE TO THIS STORY.
© 1995 United Feature Syndicate, Inc. (NYC)

6/20
AND THAT WOULD BE...?
I FORGET.

THE FINANCE DEPARTMENT HAS ANALYZED YOUR COMPUTING NEEDS AND DECIDED TO GIVE YOU A 286 PC.
S. Adams

THAT SHOULD BE SUFFICIENT FOR THE 3D-RENDERING YOU NEED TO DO.
6/21 © 1995 United Feature Syndicate, Inc. (NYC)

BESIDES, HOW MANY TIMES ARE YOU GOING TO DO 3D-RENDERING IN YOUR CAREER?
ONCE, IF I HURRY.

I RECOMMEND STANDARDIZING ON ONE TYPE OF COMPUTER FOR THE OFFICE.

WE MUST IDENTIFY AND ELIMINATE THE DEVIANT USERS OF MACINTOSH, UNIX AND . . . GOD HELP US . . . OS/2 WARP.

THE HOLY WARS BEGIN
DON'T LIE TO ME, GUSTAV! YOU'RE A STINKIN' MAC USER!!

MISTER CATBERT, THE COMPANY IS TRYING TO FORCE ME TO USE A DIFFERENT KIND OF COMPUTER.

YOU'RE THE HUMAN RESOURCES DIRECTOR. WHAT ARE YOU DOING TO STOP THIS RELIGIOUS PERSECUTION ??! WHAT EVER HAPPENED TO "DIVERSITY"??

THE LONGER YOU VERK HERE, DIVERSE IT GETS.
NEXT.

COMPUTER HOLY WARS
HOLD IT RIGHT THERE, BUDDY.

THAT SCRUFFY BEARD . . . THOSE SUSPENDERS . . . THAT SMUG EXPRESSION . . .

YOU'RE ONE OF THOSE CONDESCENDING UNIX COMPUTER USERS!
HERE'S A NICKEL, KID. GET YOURSELF A BETTER COMPUTER.

TAKE CARE OF THIS, ALICE.
"TAKE CARE OF THIS"? THIS WOULD DOUBLE MY WORKLOAD.
I'VE ALREADY GOT SO MANY PROJECTS THAT I CAN'T DO ANYTHING USEFUL WITH ANY OF THEM.
BUT IF SUCCESS IS IMPOSSIBLE THEN...
I'M...FREE.
FREE! FREE! HA HA HA HA HA
THE RESULT WILL BE THE SAME NO MATTER WHAT I DO!
YES YES YES
S. Adams
© 1995 United Feature Syndicate, Inc.
6-25

HONK HONK!
MOVING ALONG...WE NEED TO INVENTORY OUR OFFICE EQUIP-MENT.
SOUNDS LIKE A JOB FOR ALICE.

I ASKED SAINT DOGBERT TO MEDIATE OUR DISPUTE OVER WHAT KIND OF COMPUTERS ARE ALLOWED HERE.

I SHALL GO TO THE DESERT AND SEEK ENLIGHTENMENT. WHEN I RETURN I WILL REVEAL THE TRUE PATH OF COMPUTING.

PALM SPRINGS
YOU CALL THIS AN ENDORSEMENT CONTRACT?! GO TO THE END OF THE LINE!

ALICE, I WANT YOU TO BENCHMARK THESE WORLD-CLASS COMPANIES. FIND OUT HOW WE COMPARE.

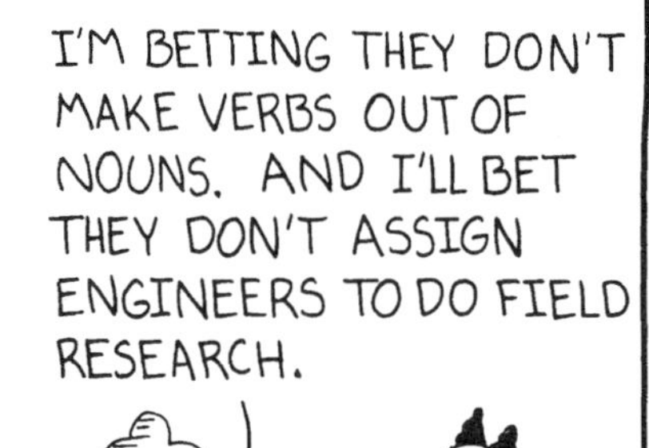
I'M BETTING THEY DON'T MAKE VERBS OUT OF NOUNS. AND I'LL BET THEY DON'T ASSIGN ENGINEERS TO DO FIELD RESEARCH.

DO YOU GUYS HAVE ANY POINTY-HAIRED IDIOTS RUNNING YOUR PLACE?
WOULD YOU LIKE ONE?

AS YOU REQUESTED, I BENCHMARKED OUR COMPANY AGAINST FIVE WORLD-CLASS COMPANIES.

THE COMPARISONS ARE IRRELEVANT BECAUSE WE'RE IN DIFFERENT INDUSTRIES. BUT THAT DIDN'T STOP ME.

WHY CAN THEY MAKE A POTATO CHIP IN ONE SECOND BUT IT TAKES US MONTHS TO DEVELOP SOFTWARE?
I THINK THEY OIL THE CHIPS.

DOGBERT THE CONSULTANT
ONE WAY TO LOOK AT YOUR PROBLEM IS THAT NOBODY LIKES YOUR PRODUCTS.

BUT I DON'T KNOW HOW TO FIX THAT. SO I RECOMMEND FORMING INTERNAL BUSINESS UNITS TO BICKER WITH EACH OTHER.
S.ADAMS

WHY WOULD YOU RECOMMEND THAT?
WELL, I'D BE LYING IF I SAID I LIKED YOU.

WE'RE GOING TO FOLLOW THE ADVICE OF THE DOGBERT CONSULTING COMPANY AND FORM "BATTLIN' BUSINESS UNITS."

WE'LL SPEND MOST OF OUR TIME CROSS-CHARGING AND UNDERMINING THE OTHER BBU'S.
S.ADAMS

A LITTLE COMPETITION IS HEALTHY.
WHATEVER YOU DO, DON'T TICK OFF THE JANITORIAL BBU.

DOGBERT THE CONSULTANT
WE TOOK YOUR ADVICE AND FORMED BUSINESS UNITS WITHIN THE COMPANY...

NOW WE SPEND ALL OF OUR TIME FIGHTING WITH EACH OTHER ABOUT WHO DOES WHAT.
S.ADAMS

WHAT EXACTLY DID YOU MEAN WHEN YOU SAID IT WOULD "GUARANTEE FUTURE BUSINESS"?
OH LOOK — MY CONTRACT JUST EXPIRED.

I'D LIKE YOU ALL TO MEET OUR NEW CO-OP EMPLOYEE.
S. Adams

WE DON'T PAY HIM. HE WORKS FOR FREE TO GAIN VALUABLE JOB EXPERIENCE.

I'M PUTTING YOU IN CHARGE OF THE PTG PROJECT!
WOW! WHAT IS IT?!!

PTG STANDS FOR "PAPER TOWEL GUY."

IF SOMEBODY SPILLS COFFEE IT'S YOUR JOB TO THROW YOUR BODY ON IT BEFORE IT REACHES ONE OF US.
7/2

OOPS

FIRE IN THE HOLE!!!

HOW'D I DO?
NOT SO GOOD, KID. THAT WAS TEA.

HA HA! NOW THAT THE ENGINEERS MUST CHARGE THEIR TIME TO MARKETING, WE OWN YOU!
S. Adams

I'LL JUST REPROGRAM YOUR COMPUTER THROUGH THE LAN SO ITS RADIATION WILL ALTER YOUR DNA.

IS THAT POSSIBLE??!
AS FAR AS YOU KNOW.

I TOLD A GUY IN MARKETING THAT I PROGRAMMED HIS COMPUTER TO ALTER HIS DNA STRUCTURE.
HEE HEE
S. Adams

HE THINKS HE'LL TURN INTO SOME KIND OF ANIMAL.
TELL HIM YOU SET IT TO "WEASEL." IT'LL TAKE LONGER TO NOTICE ANY CHANGE.

TELL ME THE TRUTH, ALICE. CAN DILBERT REPROGRAM MY DNA?
YEAH. YOU MARKETING GUYS ONLY HAVE ONE HELIX.

MAYBE YOU SHOULDN'T HAVE TOLD STAN YOU REPROGRAMMED HIS DNA THROUGH THE LAN.
S. Adams

THOSE MARKETING GUYS BELIEVE ANYTHING. THEY EVEN BELIEVE MARKET RESEARCH, FOR HEAVEN'S SAKE.

THERE'S NO TELLING WHAT THE POWER OF SUGGESTION MIGHT DO.
WELL, THANK YOU VERY MUCH.

I JOKINGLY TOLD STAN IN MARKETING THAT I REPROGRAMMED HIS DNA. HE'S SO GULLIBLE THAT HE'S ACTUALLY CHANGING!
S. Adams

YOU MUST USE HIS GULLIBILITY TO REVERSE THE PROCESS. REMEMBER, HIS ENTIRE REALITY IS SHAPED BY UNVERIFIED CUSTOMER ANECDOTES.

I HEARD A RUMOR OF A STORY OF AN ALLEGED FOCUS GROUP WHERE A QUOTE TAKEN OUT OF CONTEXT INDICATES YOU'RE NOT BECOMING A WEASEL.

I'M NOT?!
YIPEEE!

OUR NEW DRESS POLICY AT WORK ALLOWS CASUAL CLOTHES ON FRIDAYS.
S. Adams

THAT'S GOOD, BECAUSE STUDIES HAVE SHOWN THAT FRIDAYS ARE THE ONLY SAFE DAY TO DRESS CASUALLY; ANY OTHER DAY WOULD CAUSE A STOCK PLUNGE.
IS IT JUST ME OR IS THAT POLICY STUPID?
THAT'S NOT AN "OR" QUESTION.

I WANT US TO HAVE THE SAME KIND OF TEAMWORK AS THE EGYPTIANS WHO BUILT THE PYRAMIDS!
S. Adams

SOME SCHOLARS BELIEVE THE PYRAMIDS WERE BUILT BY SLAVES.

BUT THERE'S SOME DOUBT; THAT'S ALL I'M SHOOTING FOR.
I THINK THEY WERE GUIDED BY UFOs TOO.

WE DESPERATELY NEED ANOTHER PERSON ON MY PROJECT!
WE'RE ALREADY OVER HEADCOUNT. GET A CONTRACT EMPLOYEE.
OKAY, BUT THEY COST TWICE AS MUCH.
S. Adams
PLUS WE NEED TO BUY A COMPUTER.
RENT ONE. WE'RE OVER OUR CAPITAL BUDGET.
RENTING IS EXPENSIVE. WE'LL GO OVER OUR EXPENSE BUDGET.
I'LL FIRE WALLY. THAT WILL FREE UP SOME CASH.
WALLY'S ON MY PROJECT!
7/9

FORGET IT! I'LL JUST WORK SIXTEEN HOURS A DAY!!
THAT WORKED OUT PERFECTLY. I THINK I MIGHT BE A GENIUS OR SOMETHING.
I WONDER IF I SHOULD HAVE TOLD HIM THE PROJECT WAS CANCELLED LAST WEEK.

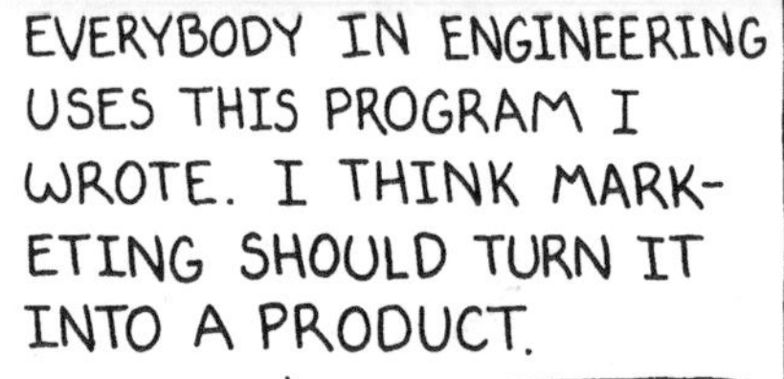
EVERYBODY IN ENGINEERING USES THIS PROGRAM I WROTE. I THINK MARKETING SHOULD TURN IT INTO A PRODUCT.

I WOULDN'T BUY THIS.

THAT'S IRRELEVANT BECAUSE THE TARGET MARKET WOULD BE ENGINEERS.
ENGINEERS THINK THE SAME AS MARKETEERS.

IF THAT WERE TRUE WE'D BE SITTING IN A CAVE TRYING TO DECIDE IF ROCKS ARE EDIBLE.
YOU KNOW, YOU COULD KEEP RECIPES ON THIS.

I AM SAINT DOGBERT. I HAVE COME TO DRIVE OUT THE STALE AND OVERUSED JOKES ABOUT THE INFORMATION SUPERHIGHWAY.

SOMETIMES I FEEL LIKE ROADKILL ON THE INFORMATION SUPERHIGHWAY!

DON'T MAKE ME COME OVER THERE!

I THINK YOU LIKE THAT COMPUTER MORE THAN YOU LIKE ME.

THAT'S NOT TRUE, LIZ. I DO NOT LIKE THAT COMPUTER MORE THAN I LIKE YOU.

PLEASE, PLEASE DON'T ASK ABOUT THE LAPTOP.
"THAT" COMPUTER?

OKAY, LET'S START BY DOCUMENTING YOUR MARKET REQUIREMENTS.
S. Adams

NO, LET'S START BY YOU TELLING ME ALL THE THINGS YOU CAN DESIGN. THEN I'LL TELL YOU WHICH ONE I LIKE.
7/3 © 1995 United Feature Syndicate, Inc. (NYC)

WORK CAN BE VERY REWARDING. YOU SHOULD TRY IT.
WHAT'S THAT DOOHICKEY YOU HAVE THERE?

CAROL, THE NEXT TIME YOU ORDER MY BUSINESS CARDS, SPELL OUT MY FULL TITLE: "DIRECTOR OF PRODUCT ENHANCEMENTS."
S. Adams

DON'T USE THE ACRONYM "DOPE."
7/14 © 1995 United Feature Syndicate, Inc. (NYC)

I DIDN'T KNOW YOU WERE THE DIRECTOR OF PRODUCT ENHANCE-MENTS.

I WANT YOU TO STUDY OUR OPTIONS FOR PROJECT "ZEBRA" AND MAKE A RECOMMENDATION.
S. Adams

TRANSLATION: "READ MY MIND THEN RECOMMEND THE OPTION I'VE ALREADY DECIDED ON."
7/15 © 1995 United Feature Syndicate, Inc. (NYC)

I'LL GET RIGHT ON IT!
TRANSLATION: "I AM DOOMED. I WILL GO LOOK FOR NAUGHTY PICTURES ON THE INTERNET INSTEAD."

I'VE DECIDED TO MAKE SOME CHANGES TO OUR CORPORATE CULTURE.
S. Adams

LET ME GUESS WHAT THAT MEANS.

WE'LL WORK LONGER HOURS WITHOUT EXTRA PAY...

YOUR MANAGEMENT STYLE WILL REMAIN EXACTLY THE SAME BECAUSE LORD KNOWS THERE'S NO NEED FOR YOU TO CHANGE.

WE'LL START CALLING OURSELVES A "TEAM" SO IT DOESN'T SEEM LIKE WORK!
7-16

I PREDICT THERE WILL BE VAPID SLOGANS PRINTED ON NOTEPADS, AND MAYBE SOME USELESS MEETINGS.
SHE'S PSYCHIC!

IS IT JUST ME OR IS THE CULTURE ALREADY CHANGING?
I FEEL IT! WE'RE CHANGING!

WHAT'S NEXT ON THE FAD MENU?
I WONDER IF IT'S TOO LATE TO RULE BY FEAR.

WHAT DID YOU BRING TO READ?
IT'S A BOOK OF TIPS FOR MY NEW COMPUTER GOLF GAME.
S. Adams

SO... YOU'RE READING A BOOK... ABOUT A COMPUTER SIMULATION... OF AN ACTIVITY THAT'S ALMOST A SPORT...

THAT'S ABOUT AS CLOSE AS YOU CAN GET TO BEING A NON-ORGANIC LIFE FORM.
THIS CHAPTER IS ABOUT DRIVING THE LITTLE CART.

THAT'S AN INTERESTING SUGGESTION, WALLY. BUT IF IT'S A GOOD IDEA, WHY AREN'T OTHER COMPANIES DOING IT?
S. Adams

CAN YOU IMAGINE IN YOUR WILDEST DREAMS THAT MAYBE, JUST MAYBE I HAD A GOOD IDEA THAT NOBODY ELSE THOUGHT OF?!!

YOU MUST HAVE SEEN IT IN A BOOK.
THANKS FOR THE CONFIDENCE IN MY ABILITIES.
YOU READ A BOOK?

I DON'T KNOW WHAT KIND OF GIFT TO BUY FOR TED'S BABY SHOWER.
S. Adams

HAND-CRAFTED ITEMS ARE GOOD. CUT THREE HOLES IN A PAPER BAG AND YOU'VE GOT A LOVELY BABY DRESS.

HE MIGHT THINK I'M CHEAP.
DO YOU THINK THE KID HAS A SALT SHAKER YET?

TED'S BABY SHOWER
OH LOOK, IT'S A STAPLER...
S. Adams

I CAN USE THIS TO TAKE UP THE HEM ON THE LOVELY HAND-CRAFTED PAPER BAG DRESS THAT DILBERT MADE.

IT LOOKS JUST LIKE THE ONE THAT DISAPPEARED FROM MY CUBICLE THIS MORNING.
EXCEPT YOURS HAD STAPLES.

IT'S REALLY DIFFERENT AROUND HERE SINCE WE LOST DILBERT'S DAD.
WHEN DID HE DIE?
S. Adams

HE'S NOT DEAD. WE LOST HIM AT THE MALL, CHRISTMAS OF '92.

SHOULDN'T YOU BE LOOKING FOR HIM?
I SAID IT'S DIFFERENT, NOT WORSE.

I CAN'T BELIEVE YOUR FATHER HAS BEEN LOST AT THE MALL SINCE 1992!
S. Adams

IF MY FATHER OR MY HUSBAND WERE LOST AT THE MALL I'D BE SEARCHING FOR HIM TWENTY-FOUR HOURS A DAY!!

WE'RE WAITING FOR A SALE.
YOU'RE A BIT OF A WHINER, AREN'T YOU, DEAR?

I HAD A FEW SUGGESTIONS ON YOUR DOCUMENT, ALICE.
S.Adams
THANKS
BONK
I'VE MADE SOME UPGRADES TO YOUR DOCUMENT, ALICE.
THAT'S JUST WHAT IT NEEDED: A BUNCH OF OBTUSE ACRONYMS AND JARGON.
OOOH, LOOKY! YOU'VE ALSO MADE ELEGANT MULTI-TOPIC SENTENCES OUT OF MY STUBBY CLEAR ONES!
7/23
THANK YOU. AND PUT ME DOWN AS THE AUTHOR SINCE I'M THE BOSS.
MAYBE I SHOULD DISTRIBUTE LITTLE PLASTIC STATUES OF YOU WITH EVERY COPY. HOW ABOUT THAT?
HERE'S YOUR COPY, HERE'S YOUR STATUE, DON'T ASK.
OUR QUALITY IS LOW, BUT AT LEAST WE DON'T GET CREDIT.

AS USUAL, THE BOSS IS LATE. WHAT DO YOU WANT TO DO?
S. Adams

LET'S PRACTICE MAKING SMALL TALK. IT'LL COME IN HANDY WHEN WE MEET WITH MARKETING.

SO, ALICE, HAVEN'T WE SEEN THAT OUTFIT A LOT?
THIS CHAIR IS SPRINGY. DO YOU THINK THEY'RE ALL SPRINGY?

IT'S AMAZING HOW MUCH WE'VE CHANGED SINCE PREHISTORIC TIMES.
S. Adams

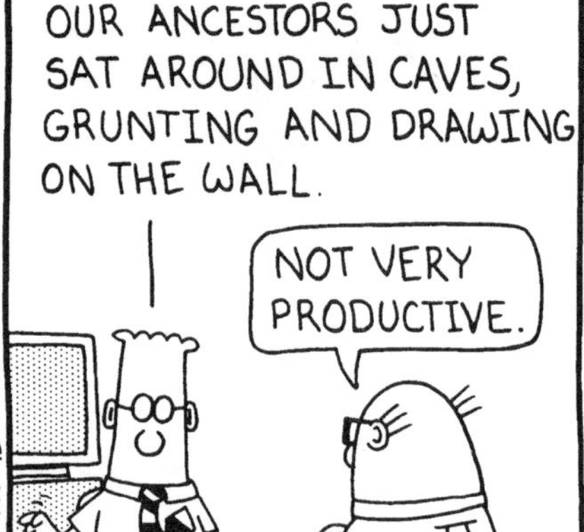
OUR ANCESTORS JUST SAT AROUND IN CAVES, GRUNTING AND DRAWING ON THE WALL.
NOT VERY PRODUCTIVE.

IT WAS JUST THIS, ALL DAY LONG.
MMM. YUP.

MY PROPOSED WORK PLAN FOR THE YEAR IS TO STRESS-TEST OUR PRODUCT UNDER SEVERE NETWORK CONDITIONS.
S. Adams

I WILL ACCOMPLISH THIS BY DOWNLOADING LARGE IMAGE FILES FROM THE BUSIEST SERVERS ON THE NET.

I WAS THIS CLOSE TO MAKING IT MY JOB TO DOWNLOAD NAUGHTY PICTURES.
IT'S JUST AS WELL; I WOULD HAVE HAD TO KILL YOU.

BOB, YOUR SELF-ESTEEM MIGHT IMPROVE IF YOU GOT A JOB.
AS WHAT?

THERE'S AN OPENING IN OUR PROCUREMENT DEPARTMENT. YOU'D BE PERFECT.
WHAT DOES PROCURE-MENT DO?

THEIR JOB IS TO PREVENT US FROM GETTING THE COMPUTERS WE WANT.
CAN I HIT PEOPLE WITH MY TAIL?

BOB WORKS IN PROCUREMENT
YOUR DUTIES ARE SIMPLE. PEOPLE WILL COME TO YOU AND ASK FOR THINGS.

ASSUME ALL EMPLOYEES ARE LYING, TREASURE-HUNTING THIEVES. GIVE THEM LOW-COST SUB-STITUTES AND CLAIM THE SAVINGS ON YOUR ACCOMPLISHMENTS.

I ASKED FOR A MULTIMEDIA LAPTOP PC. THIS IS A "DYMO" LABELER.
NICE TRY, PAUL, IF THAT'S YOUR REAL NAME.

BOB IN PROCUREMENT
I'M AFRAID THE EQUIP-MENT YOU WANT IS NOT ON THE APPROVED EQUIPMENT LIST.

LET ME THINK... IF I ADD THIS TO THE APPROVED LIST, THAT'S MORE WORK FOR ME... BUT IF I SAY NO, IT'S MORE WORK FOR YOU... HMM...THINK, THINK...

I'D LIKE TO SEE THIS ALLEGED LIST.
WELL, IT'S NOT SO MUCH A PHYSICAL LIST AS IT IS A PHILOSOPHY.

OUR NEW VP SAYS HE HAS AN "OPEN DOOR POLICY." LET'S CHECK IT OUT.
S. ADAMS
KNOCK KNOCK
HI HO. NOTHING IMPORTANT. WE JUST WANTED TO DROP IN.
THIS OPEN DOOR POLICY IS GREAT. OUR LAST VP WAS ALOOF.
ARE THOSE SOURBALLS?
LOOK AT ALL THE FURNITURE IN HERE!
I CALL COUCH!
IS THERE SOMETHING I CAN DO FOR YOU?
WELL... SOMETIMES OUR CUBICLES ARE TOO HOT.
COULD YOU HAVE SOMEBODY LOOK INTO IT?
7-30 © 1995 United Feature Syndicate, Inc.
BOY, THOSE SOURBALLS SURE LULL YOU INTO A FALSE SENSE OF SECURITY.
THE MAN IS LIKE A HUGE INSINCERE SPIDER.

I THINK, THEREFORE I AM.

BUT I'M MICROMANAGED, THEREFORE I AM NOT.
S. Adams

I HAVE A PHILOSOPHICAL QUESTION FOR YOU.
YOU'RE NOT ME, THEREFORE YOU'RE IRRELEVANT.

WE'RE PLANNING TO HIRE A TEMP AT WORK. YOU SHOULD APPLY FOR THE JOB, RATBERT.
WOW! ME? A TEMP?!

AS A TEMP I WOULD FINALLY GET ALL OF THE RESPECT AND UNCONDITIONAL LOVE THAT I DESERVE!!
S. Adams

DANGER: SHARP LEARNING CURVE AHEAD.
I ASSUME I'LL GET AN OFFICE AND A SECRETARY.

I SUBMIT MYSELF AS A CANDIDATE FOR THE POSITION OF "TEMPORARY EMPLOYEE."
S. Adams

I'M VERY TEMPORARY. FIRST I'LL BE IN ONE PLACE AND THEN YOU BLINK AND I'M GONE! BLINK, GONE, BLINK, GONE, BLINK, GONE...

STOP SAYING "BLINK, GONE." IT'S MAKING ME NUTS.
IT APPEARS THAT THE BALANCE OF POWER HAS SHIFTED MY WAY.

CONGRATULATIONS ON GETTING HIRED AS A TEMP, RATBERT.
WHERE DO I START?!
S. Adams

YOUR OFFICE IS THIS CARDBOARD BOX IN THE MAIN HALLWAY. THE REGULAR EMPLOYEES WILL NOT MAKE EYE CONTACT OR ASK YOUR NAME.
YOUR STATUS IS ROUGHLY BETWEEN THE SECURITY GUARD AND THE CRUD BEHIND THE REFRIGERATOR.
DO I GET A COMPANY CAR?

RATBERT THE TEMP WORKER
THIS IS REALLY TESTING MY SENSE OF SELF-WORTH.
S. Adams

I WILL COMPENSATE BY SHOUTING A LIST OF MY TALENTS TO ANYBODY WHO WALKS PAST.

IGNORE HIM. HE'S TRYING TO TRICK US INTO MAKING EYE CONTACT.
I EAT RUBBER! I CARRY DISEASE! I ENJOY OPERA!

RATBERT THE TEMP WORKER
I'M ONLY A TEMP, BUT I DEMAND RESPECT!!
S. Adams

OKAY, MAYBE THAT'S TOO MUCH TO ASK. BUT I DEMAND THAT SOMEBODY MAKE EYE CONTACT WITH ME!!

HOW'S THIS?
THAT'S PERIPHERAL VISION!!!

WHEN DID YOU START BELIEVING THAT YOUR BOSS WAS AN EVIL ENTITY FROM ANOTHER DIMENSION?
S.Adams

I'D LIKE TO SIT IN ON YOUR CUSTOMER MEETING.
UH-OH

LET ME SHARE THE HIGH LEVEL STRATEGIC VIEW.
HERE WE GO.

LIFE BEGAN IN THE PRIMORDIAL STEW LITERALLY HUNDREDS OF YEARS AGO...

BUT WE ARE THE ONLY COMPANY WHO EVER FOUND SYNERGIES IN OUR WIN-WIN SOLUTIONS!
© 1996 United Feature Syndicate, Inc. (NYC)
8/6

TWO HOURS LATER
AND WE WON'T STOP UNTIL WE DELIGHT EVERY CUSTOMER!

I'D BE DELIGHTED IF YOU JUST TOLD ME ABOUT YOUR NEW INTERNET ACCESS PRODUCT.
I CANCELLED THE FUNDING YESTER-DAY.

WHO'S UP FOR A TOUR OF OUR CUBICLES?
GOTTA GO.

CATBERT THE HR DIRECTOR
I THINK I'LL INVENT SOME ILLOGICAL POLICIES TO ANNOY EMPLOYEES.
S. Adams

MY DIABOLICAL NEW DRESS CODE WILL MAKE THEM QUESTION THEIR OWN SANITY.

... SO, CASUAL CLOTHES DON'T LOWER OUR STOCK VALUE... BUT ONLY IF WORN ON FRIDAYS... UNLESS SOMEBODY SEES US... GOT IT?
I THINK I'M INSANE.

I DON'T UNDERSTAND YOUR NEW DRESS CODE POLICY, MR. CATBERT.
MAYBE YOU'RE INSANE.
S. Adams

IT'S SIMPLE. FRIDAYS ARE "CASUAL." BUT YOU CAN'T WEAR JEANS BECAUSE JEANS LOOK GOOD AND FEEL GOOD AND YOU ALREADY OWN SEVERAL PAIRS.

IT'S ANOTHER SADISTIC HUMAN RESOURCES PLOT TO MAKE PEOPLE QUIT!!
SAY HELLO TO UNSIGHTLY PANTY LINES.

WELL, IT WOULDN'T BE FRIDAY IF I DIDN'T SEE ALICE WEARING HER ONE PAIR OF TAN PANTS.
S. Adams

I LOVE THE "BUSINESS CASUAL" LOOK FOR THE WAY IT COMBINES UNATTRACTIVE WITH UNPROFESSIONAL WHILE DIMINISHING NEITHER.

DO YOU THINK THE FASHION OPINION OF A MALE ENGINEER MATTERS TO ME??
TWINS!

MY PLAN IS TO MAKE YOU A SELF-DIRECTED TEAM.

AFTER A FEW TEAM MEETINGS, THE DISRESPECT YOU HAVE FOR EACH OTHER WILL FESTER AND GROW INTO FULL-BLOWN LOATHING.
S. Adams

YOU'LL BEG ME TO MICRO-MANAGE YOU!! HA HA HA!!
IT ACTUALLY FEELS GOOD TO HAVE A PLAN.

I'M REORGANIZING THE DEPARTMENT INTO FAST-MOVING TEAMS.

GOOD PLAN. WE'LL NEVER REALIZE WE'RE POWERLESS, MICRO-MANAGED SERFS AFTER WE CALL OURSELVES A "TEAM."
S. Adams

I NEED SOME LESS EXPERI-ENCED PEOPLE.
I FEEL FASTER ALREADY.
THE G-FORCES ARE KILLING ME.

AS YOU REQUESTED, I DROPPED EVERYTHING AND WROTE MY CAREER DEVELOPMENT PLAN.

I PLAN TO BOUNCE FROM ONE ARTIFICIAL EMERGEN-CY TO ANOTHER, LIKE A PING-PONG BALL IN A CLOTHES DRYER, UNTIL ONE DAY I RESIGN.
S. Adams

HERE I'M USING HUMOR TO MAKE A POINT...
FAX THIS TO HR NOW!!

HERE'S HOW YOUR MARKETING DEPARTMENT CAN HELP RETAIN YOUR BEST ENGINEERS.
S. Adams

MARKETING GETS AN IDEA
WE'LL LEVERAGE OUR TECHNOLOGY BY BUILDING ANT FARMS.

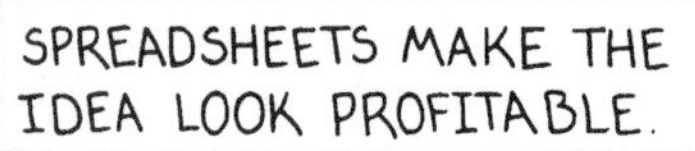
SPREADSHEETS MAKE THE IDEA LOOK PROFITABLE.

THE ANT MILK ALONE WILL BE A POSITIVE NPV!
WOW!
WHAT'S AN NPV?

DON'T FORGET THE "WORST CASE SCENARIO."
WORST CASE, SOMEBODY BUILDS A GIGANTIC MAGNIFYING GLASS NEXT DOOR...

SOLUTION: BITE-SIZED ANT JERKY!
THERE'S NO RISK!
$$$
© 1995 United Feature Syndicate, Inc. (NYC)
8/13

AN ENGINEER WILL BE ASSIGNED TO THE PROJECT.
ANT FARMS! DO IT!
UH-OH.

THE ENGINEER WILL CHALLENGE THE ASSUMPTIONS
YOU CAN'T GET A GALLON OF MILK FROM AN ANT!
WHAT DO YOU KNOW ABOUT MARKETING?

RESULT: THE ENGINEER WILL NEVER LEAVE THE COMPANY.
SO... YOUR CURRENT JOB IS "ANT FARM ENGINEER"?
I'M DOOMED.

MY STATUS FOR THE WEEK IS THAT THE ONGOING DEHUMANIZATION FROM MY JOB HAS CAUSED ME TO DOUBT MY EXISTENCE.

THERE IS REASON TO BELIEVE I AM BECOMING INVISIBLE.
S. Adams

DO I HEAR YOUR PAGER BUZZING, WALLY?
I DOUBT IT; I DON'T KEEP BATTERIES IN IT.
PLINK

THE DEHUMANIZATION OF MY JOB HAS RENDERED ME INVISIBLE TO HUMANS. ONLY YOU CAN SEE ME, DOGBERT.

HOW CAN WE FIX THIS?
YOU COULD WEAR A BAG ON YOUR HEAD WHEN YOU'RE AROUND ME.

THAT'S NOT THE FIX I HAD IN MIND.
IT'S NOT A PERFECT SOLUTION. I'D STILL BE ABLE TO HEAR YOU.

YOU'RE INVISIBLE TO YOUR CO-WORKERS. BUT YOU CAN COMPENSATE BY FORMING A SYMBIOTIC RELATIONSHIP WITH A VISIBLE CREATURE.

RATBERT WILL CLING TO YOUR BACK. HE'LL BE YOUR VISUAL AND AUDITORY LINK WITH YOUR CO-WORKERS.

SO... WORKING HARD? OR HARDLY WORKING?
I KNEW THIS COLOMBIAN COFFEE WAS TROUBLE.

DON'T BE ALARMED. I'M NOT REALLY A RAT FLOATING IN MIDAIR.
S. Adams

I'M CLINGING TO THE BACK OF AN EMPLOYEE WHO HAS BEEN RENDERED INVISIBLE BY A LONG SUCCESSION OF WORTHLESS ASSIGNMENTS.

LOOKS LIKE AN ISOLATED CASE OF BAD ATTITUDE.
WHICH ROOM IS THE "QUALITY" MEETING IN?

I SIGNIFICANTLY INCREASED MY VISIBILITY AT WORK TODAY, DOGBERT.
S. Adams

YESTERDAY I WAS INVISIBLE TO MY MANAGEMENT. BUT TODAY I AM KNOWN BY ALL.

YOU SCREWED UP, HUH?
OOH YEAH. BIG TIME.

I KNOW WHERE YOU'RE GOING.
S. Adams

YOU'RE GOING TO A MEETING WHERE EQUALLY UNINFORMED MANAGERS WILL MAKE DECISIONS THAT NEUTER THE WORK I DID ALL WEEK.

YOU DIDN'T DO ANY WORK THIS WEEK.
I THINK I'VE GOT THIS WHOLE "WORK" CONCEPT FIGURED OUT.

PLEASE DON'T PROMISE THE PRODUCT MANAGER MORE THAN WE CAN DELIVER.
S. Adams

WE NEED A TOTALLY NEW SOFTWARE INTERFACE IN ONE MONTH.
YOU GOT IT!

AND REWRITE THE OPERATING SYSTEM SO WE DOMINATE THE INDUSTRY.
CONCURRENT DEVELOPMENT.
CHECK

SUDDENLY I FEEL OMNIPOTENT.

I WANT ALL NEW HARDWARE, ANTI-GRAVITY PACKAGING, HOLOGRAPHIC AGENTS...
YAWN YAWN
8/20

CAN YOUR TEAM REALLY DO THAT IN A MONTH?
LET ME GET THEIR REACTION.

AAAGH!!

PESSIMISM WILL NOT LOOK GOOD ON YOUR PERFORMANCE REVIEW.
TWITCH

YOUR EXPENSE REPORT WAS REJECTED BY ACCOUNTING.
WHY?
S. Adams

BECAUSE THE EMPTINESS OF THEIR SHALLOW LIVES MAKES THEM WANT TO HURT OTHERS IN ORDER TO VALIDATE THEIR PATHETIC EXISTENCE.

CAN YOU HELP ME CLEAR THIS UP?
TO BE HONEST, I'M KINDA BUYING IN TO THEIR PHILOSOPHY.

IF IT'S OKAY, I'LL HOLD ONTO MY SOUL WHILE I VISIT THE ACCOUNTING DEPARTMENT.
SOUL CHECK
TIPS
S. Adams

I CAME TO ANSWER YOUR QUESTIONS ABOUT MY EXPENSE REPORT.
TAKE A SEAT.

I DON'T LIKE THE WAY THIS IS STARTING.

DILBERT'S EXPENSE VOUCHER
WHAT ARE YOU TRYING TO PULL?? DO YOU THINK WE'RE IDIOTS IN ACCOUNTING?!!
S. Adams

NO, I SWEAR, I THINK YOU'RE SMART BUT SADISTIC TROLLS WITH MANY HUMANOID CHARACTERISTICS.

APPARENTLY THERE WAS NO RIGHT ANSWER.

DILBERT'S EXPENSE VOUCHER
YOU SPENT NEARLY $10 PER DAY ON MEALS DURING YOUR TRIP.
S. Adams

THE TRAVEL GUIDELINES REQUIRE YOU TO STUN A PIGEON WITH YOUR BRIEFCASE ON THE WAY TO THE HOTEL THEN FRY IT UP ON YOUR TRAVEL IRON.
8/24 © 1995 United Feature Syndicate, Inc. (NYC)

I TRIED... BUT IT WAS TAKING SO LONG.
TRY THE "WOOL" SETTING.

DILBERT IS TRAPPED IN THE BOWELS OF ACCOUNTING
I UNDERSTAND YOU HAVE DILBERT IN THERE. FREE HIM, OR ELSE...
ELSE WHAT?
S. Adams

OR ELSE I WILL PUT THIS CAP ON MY HEAD BACKWARDS! YOUR LITTLE HARDWIRED ACCOUNTING BRAIN WILL EXPLODE JUST LOOKING AT IT.
8/25 © 1995 United Feature Syndicate, Inc. (NYC)

WHAT WAS THAT POPPING SOUND?
A PARADIGM SHIFTING WITHOUT A CLUTCH.

SOMETIMES I FEEL SELF-CONSCIOUS BECAUSE MY BRAIN IS SO TINY.
S. Adams

HERE, LET ME REACH IN MY EAR AND PULL IT OUT.
8/26 © 1995 United Feature Syndicate, Inc. (NYC)

I THINK THAT'S EAR WAX, BOB.
MAYBE. BUT I'M PUTTING IT BACK JUST IN CASE.

I MADE A FEW CHANGES TO THE DESIGN.
S. Adams

WE'LL HAVE TO WORK AROUND THE CLOCK FOR MONTHS TO MAKE THESE CHANGES!!

WORK SMARTER, NOT HARDER.

YOU'RE TRYING TO VIOLATE THE LAWS OF PHYSICS!

RULES WERE MADE TO BE BROKEN.
8/27
© 1995 United Feature Syndicate, Inc. (NYC)

THIS DESIGN WOULD CREATE ENOUGH RADIATION TO INSTANTLY KILL THE USER!!

BE SURE TO MENTION THAT IN THE DOCU-MENTATION.

LET'S WORK SMARTER NOT HARDER.
I THINK WE FOUND THE ONLY "BETA" TESTER WE'LL NEED.

TINA, YOU'LL HAVE TO HAVE ALL THE DOCUMENTATION WRITTEN BY NEXT WEEK SO WE CAN SHIP IT WHEN THE SOFTWARE IS DONE.
S. Adams

HOW CAN I WRITE INSTRUCTIONS FOR SOMETHING THAT DOESN'T EXIST YET?
YOU'LL HAVE TO MAKE LOGICAL GUESSES.

"IF YOU PRESS ANY KEY YOUR COMPUTER WILL LOCK UP. IF YOU CALL OUR TECH SUPPORT WE'LL BLAME 'MICROSOFT.'"

I FEEL LIKE TWEAKING SOME BRITTLE PEOPLE. DO YOU KNOW ANY BRITTLE PEOPLE?
S. Adams

TRY TINA THE TECH WRITER. SHE BELIEVES THAT ALL FORMS OF EXPRESSION ARE AN INSULT TO HER GENDER AND HER PROFESSION.

THE STATUE OF "VENUS DE MILO" HAS NO ARMS.
OH, I GET IT. YOU'RE SAYING THAT WOMEN CAN'T LIFT HEAVY OBJECTS.

DOGBERT TWEAKS TINA THE BRITTLE TECH WRITER.
WHAT DO YOU THINK OF THE MOVIE "THELMA AND LOUISE"?
S. Adams

I KNOW WHAT YOU'RE TRYING TO SAY. YOU THINK ALL WOMEN ARE BAD DRIVERS. THAT'S REALLY THE POINT OF THE MOVIE, ISN'T IT??

IF YOU'RE NOT OFFENDED YET, TUNE IN TOMORROW.
THE "THREE STOOGES"?
WHY ARE ALL OF THE DOCUMENTARIES ABOUT MEN??!

DOGBERT TWEAKS TINA THE BRITTLE TECH WRITER
IS TECHNICAL WRITING THE SAME AS WORD PROCESSING?
NO!!!

I AM A HIGHLY SKILLED COMMUNICATIONS PROFESSIONAL! I CAN TAKE JUMBLES OF INERT THOUGHTS AND BRING THEM TO LIFE!!
S. Adams
8/31 © 1995 United Feature Syndicate, Inc.(NYC)

MY SECRETARY IS RUNNING THE STAFF MEETING. I NEED YOU TO RETYPE THIS ORG CHART.
THE DOCTOR IS IN!

THIS WEEK WE INTRODUCED TINA THE BRITTLE TECH WRITER TO THE STRIP. TINA IS DYSFUNCTIONAL LIKE EVERYBODY HERE EXCEPT ME.
RRRR

SEND YOUR OPINIONS BY E-MAIL TO SCOTTADAMS@AOL.COM
IT'S THE ONLY WAY WE CAN LEARN.
RRRR
S. Adams
9/1 © 1995 United Feature Syndicate, Inc.(NYC)

PICK ONE
A. WOMEN SHOULD ONLY BE PORTRAYED AS LAWYERS AND STARSHIP CAPTAINS.
B. I DON'T HAVE E-MAIL.
C. TINA SHOULD BE TREATED WITH THE SAME DIGNITY AS DILBERT AND WALLY.
D. TAKE AN ART CLASS.

RECORDS RETENTION

THESE VALUABLE DOCUMENTS SHOULD BE STORED FOR FIVE YEARS.
S. Adams
9/2 © 1995 United Feature Syndicate, Inc.(NYC)

THIS JOB GOT SO MUCH EASIER WHEN I REALIZED THAT NOBODY EVER ASKS FOR ANYTHING BACK.

MY LAPTOP PC KEEPS FREEZING UP. COME TAKE A LOOK AT IT.
I'M TELECOMMUTING, DOGBERT. I CAN'T BE DISTRACTED BY HOME PROJECTS.
S. Adams
DON'T COME ANOTHER STEP CLOSER. THIS IS MY VIRTUAL CUBICLE, WITHIN WHICH I CAN NOT BE DISTURBED.
THESE INVISIBLE WALLS FORM A CONE OF PRODUCTIVITY AROUND ME.
WITHIN THIS ZONE I AM A DEDICATED EMPLOYEE, TOTALLY FOCUSED ON THE CORPORATE VISION.
9/3
© 1995 United Feature Syndicate, Inc.(NYC)
NOTHING CAN DISTRACT ME FROM MY FIRM COMMITMENT TO THE WORK-AT-HOME PRINCIPLE.
FINE. I THINK I'LL SET THE COUCH ON FIRE.
ANOTHER VICTORY FOR THE DISTRACTOR!
I SWEAR, SOMEDAY PRINCIPLE WILL WIN!

PROFITS ARE DOWN, MORALE IS SINKING; IT'S TIME FOR BOLD LEADERSHIP!!

SO I GOT SOME INSPIRATIONAL POSTERS FEATURING A VARIETY OF RELEVANT NATURE SCENES.

I THINK YOU CAN RELATE TO THIS SCENE.
AM I THE SEAGULL OR THE CLAM?

MY NEW INSPIRATIONAL POSTER IS SO EFFECTIVE THAT I DECIDED TO CARRY IT WITH ME.

WHAT DO YOU THINK, ALICE? ARE YOU INSPIRED?
I'D REALLY HAVE TO SEE THE FRONT...

HMM... I DON'T THINK THERE'S A WIN-WIN SCENARIO HERE...
TELL ME ABOUT IT...

MY INSPIRATIONAL POSTERS AREN'T WORKING. I NEED TO DO SOME ANIMAL RESEARCH, RATBERT.
READY!!
IN THIS BEAUTIFUL SCENE WE SEE A MIGHTY EAGLE SWOOPING DOWN TO CAPTURE ITS PREY. WHAT IS YOUR REACTION?

I THINK IT'S WORKING.
RUN FOR IT, MOM!!!

I SHOULD QUIT AND BECOME A CONTRACT EMPLOYEE. THEN I'D HAVE MORE INCOME AND I'D FEEL THE WIND IN MY HAIR.
S. Adams

IT'S POSSIBLE YOU'D HAVE NO INCOME AT ALL...

AND IF YOU WANT WIND IN YOUR HAIR YOU'LL HAVE TO TAKE OFF YOUR SHIRT AND RUN AROUND WITH YOUR ARMS UP.
THANK YOU FOR YOUR SUPPORT.

ALICE, I'M THINKING ABOUT QUITTING AND BECOMING A CONTRACT EMPLOYEE. DO YOU HAVE ANY ADVICE?
S. Adams

SLEEP IN DOORWAYS SO IT DOESN'T RAIN ON YOU. THE BEST SHOPPING CARTS ARE AT "LUCKY." YOU CAN MAKE AN EXCELLENT SIGN WITH A BLACK MARKING PEN AND A HUNK OF CARDBOARD.

I HATE ALL OF MY CO-WORKERS.
DESPITE THE NAME, FOOD STAMPS ARE NOT EDIBLE.

I NEED TO THINK "OUTSIDE THE BOX" TO COME UP WITH A CREATIVE DESIGN...
S. Adams

I PUSH MY CHAIR INTO THE HALLWAY TO CHANGE MY VIEWPOINT AND STIMULATE MY CREATIVE JUICES.

SUDDENLY MY JUICE DRIES UP.
YOU'RE A FIRE HAZARD. DO YOUR THINKING INSIDE YOUR BOX.

WE JUST HIRED JACK AWAY FROM OUR COMPETITOR. HE WAS THEIR BEST MANAGER.
S. ADAMS

JACK WILL BE IN CHARGE OF PROJECT "GOOSEFOOD."

I'D LIKE YOU TWO TO BRIEF JACK ON THE PROJECT.

PROJECT "GOOSEFOOD" HAS NO BUDGET AND NO MANAGEMENT SUPPORT.

YOUR JOB IS TO BUILD A GLOBAL INFORMATION NETWORK IN TWO WEEKS.

FAILURE IS CERTAIN. SOON YOU WILL LEAVE THE INDUSTRY IN DISGRACE.
9/10

... JUST LIKE THE OTHER "BEST MANAGERS" WE HIRED FROM OUR COMPETITORS.

JUST OUT OF CURIOSITY, HOW DID THE PROJECT GET ITS NAME?
LET'S JUST SAY THAT YOU'RE THE GOOSE FOOD...

AS DIRECTOR OF HUMAN RESOURCES I'VE BEEN ASKED TO REDUCE THE COST OF EMPLOYEE BENEFITS.
S. Adams

THE COMPANY WILL NO LONGER PAY FOR EYE-GLASSES. BUT WE WILL SUPPORT A NEW VISION-CORRECTION PROCEDURE.
9/11

RADIAL KERATOTOMY?
SQUINTING.

I HAVE TO CUT JANITOR EXPENSES. DO YOU THINK I'LL HAVE ANY HR ISSUES IF I MAKE EMPLOYEES EMPTY THEIR OWN TRASH?
S. Adams

WE'LL SOFTEN THE BAD NEWS BY SIMULTANEOUSLY INTRODUCING A NEW EMPLOYEE FITNESS PROGRAM...
9/12

OKAY, EVERYBODY, IT'S TIME TO TRASHERCISE!!!

I'M WRITING AN E-MAIL TO PROTEST THE NEW POLICY OF MAKING THE EMPLOYEES EMPTY THEIR OWN TRASH AT NIGHT.
S. Adams

IT'S STUPID TO HAVE HIGHLY PAID ENGINEERS DOING UNPRODUCTIVE TASKS WHEN WE COULD BE INVENTING THE FUTURE!
9/13

ARE YOU COMING TO THE "QUALITY FAIRE"?
NO, THIS WILL TAKE ANOTHER HOUR.

HERE'S THE PROBLEM. WE'VE GOT A WHOLE NEST OF PAPER TROLLS.
S. Adams

AAIIEE!

IF I CALL 911 NOW I'LL NEVER KNOW IF THE LOWER PAPER TRAY WOULD HAVE WORKED.

HERE'S MY TIME SHEET, FILLED OUT IN INCREMENTS OF FIFTEEN MINUTES.
S. Adams

AS USUAL, I CODED THE USELESS HOURS SPENT IN MEETINGS AS "WORK," WHEREAS THE TIME I SPENT IN THE SHOWER DESIGNING CIRCUITS IN MY MIND IS "NON-WORK."

INTERESTINGLY, EVEN THE TIME I SPEND COMPLAINING ABOUT MY LACK OF PRODUCTIVITY IS CONSIDERED "WORK."
I HATE MY LIFE.

IF THE DEPARTMENT MEETS ITS GOAL FOR THE QUARTER YOU CAN SHAVE MY HEAD!
S. Adams

THAT WOULD BE A BIG IMPROVEMENT.
HE'S TRYING TO SAVE MONEY ON A HAIRCUT
IF WE DOUBLE OUR GOAL CAN WE IRON YOUR SHIRT, TOO?
I NEED SOME LESS EXPERIENCED EMPLOYEES.

IT'S TIME FOR MARKETING TO PUT THE GLITTER ON THIS SOFTWARE YOU'VE CREATED.
S. Adams

WITH MY GUIDANCE THIS WILL BECOME THE PREMIER DATA BACKUP SOFTWARE!

BEAR IN MIND THAT WE SAID IT WOULD TAKE SIX MONTHS TO WRITE IT.
YOU ONLY GAVE US A MONTH.

WE'LL FIX THE BUGS IN THE NEXT RELEASE.
TELL ME ABOUT THE FEATURES.

AT THIS POINT ALL IT DOES IS ERASE YOUR DISK DRIVE.
UNLESS YOU'RE ON A NETWORK.

WHAT HAPPENS IF YOU'RE ON A NETWORK?
IT ERASES EVERYBODY'S DISK DRIVES.
9/17

AND HEAVEN HELP YOU IF YOU HAVE A MODEM...
IT CALLS ALL YOUR FRIENDS AND ERASES THEIR PCs.

WE'LL CALL IT "QuikProtect."
IF YOU HAVE A SOUND CARD IT SWEARS AT YOU.

WHERE ARE YOU TAKING ALL OF THAT OFFICE EQUIPMENT?
I'M HAVING A GARAGE SALE.
S. Adams

OUR NEW COMPANY SLOGAN IS "ACT LIKE YOU OWN THE COMPANY." SO I'VE BEEN SELLING THE STUFF THAT I DON'T USE AND KEEPING THE MONEY.

IS THAT MY NEW COLOR MONITOR?
YEAH, I NEVER USED THAT THING.

I'M HAPPY TO REPORT THAT I HAVE EMBRACED THE NEW COMPANY SLOGAN "ACT LIKE YOU OWN THE COMPANY."
S. Adams

THIS MORNING I FIRED THE MARKETING DEPARTMENT AND HAD SECURITY ESCORT THEM OUT.

THAT'S NOT EXACTLY WHAT WE HAD IN MIND...
FORTUNATELY I ANTICIPATED YOUR REACTION.

PRESS "ONE" FOR SALES. PRESS "TWO" IN A HOPELESS EFFORT TO GET TECHNICAL SUPPORT.
2
S. Adams

PRESS "ONE" FOR ANSWERS TO QUESTIONS YOU DON'T HAVE. PRESS "TWO" IF YOU'RE GULLIBLE AND OPTIMISTIC.
2

PRESS "TWO" IF YOU'RE WILLING TO BUY SOMETHING JUST SO YOU CAN TALK TO A HUMAN BEING...

I'VE BEEN ON HOLD FOR TECH SUPPORT SINCE TUESDAY. GET BOB AND MEET ME IN THE CAR.
S. ADAMS

I CAN'T WAIT TO TRY MY NEWEST MANEUVER, THE "TURBAN WEDGIE."

IT STARTS LIKE A REGULAR WEDGIE THEN I WRAP IT AROUND HIS HEAD.
QUESTION...

ALICE, I'VE DECIDED TO ADD A RESOURCE TO YOUR PROJECT.
S. ADAMS

WE'RE HUMAN BEINGS, NOT "RESOURCES"!!

WOULD IT HELP IF I TOLD YOU THAT RESOURCES ARE OUR MOST VALUABLE ASSET?

I FOUND SOFTWARE THAT HELPS MANAGERS WRITE PERFORMANCE EVALUATIONS!
UH-OH
S. ADAMS

IT'S MADE BY THE SAME COMPANY THAT MAKES FORTUNE COOKIES FOR CANADA!
THAT MAKES ME FEEL BETTER.

NEXT DAY
"DON'T BUY A NEW CAR."
I DIDN'T THINK YOU KNEW HOW TO USE A PC.
MY SECRETARY WROTE THESE.

I HAVE TO TAKE A CONTRACT TO OUR COMPANY LAWYER. I NEED YOUR HELP, DOGBERT.
S. Adams
GIVE ME ALL OF YOUR COPIES PLUS THE ORIGINAL. THEN GO AWAY.

PLEASE REVIEW THIS CONTRACT. I NEED IT TODAY.

DON'T DO IT! HE PLANS TO LOSE THEM!!
GOOD DOG!
DANG!

I CANNOT APPROVE THIS. SOMEBODY MIGHT SUE US FOR NO GOOD REASON.

9/24

THAT'S TRUE WITH ANY CONTRACT. ISN'T HE USING ABSURD LOGIC?
LET'S FIND OUT.

APPROVE THE CONTRACT NOW OR I'LL SUE YOU FOR OBSTRUCTION OF DOGS!!
OKAY OKAY

WOW
THE GREAT THING ABOUT ABSURD LOGIC IS THAT IT FITS ANY SITUATION.

WE'RE HAVING AN ISO 9000 AUDIT THIS WEEK.
S. Adams

TAKE A LOOK AT YOUR DOCUMENTED JOB DESCRIPTIONS AND MAKE SURE THAT IT'S WHAT YOU'RE DOING IF THE AUDITOR ASKS.
ACCORDING TO THIS I'M SOME SORT OF ENGINEER.
AS IF WE'D HAVE TIME FOR THAT...

I'VE BEEN HIRED BY YOUR COMPANY TO PERFORM AN ISO 9000 AUDIT.
S. Adams

BASICALLY, YOU GIVE ME MONEY AND I TELL YOU THAT YOU'RE A BUNCH OF DOLTS. IT'S THE PERFECT JOB FOR ME.
TELL ME WHAT YOU DO HERE, ALICE, IF THAT'S YOUR REAL NAME.
I'M AN ENGINEER. I MAKE SLIDES THAT PEOPLE CAN'T READ. SOMETIMES I EAT DONUTS.

HERE ARE THE RESULTS OF MY ISO 9000 AUDIT OF YOUR COMPANY.
S. Adams
YOUR EMPLOYEES ARE LARGELY UNTRAINED AND – I COULDN'T HELP NOTICE – FAIRLY UNATTRACTIVE.
HOWEVER, THEY ARE ALSO HIGHLY SKILLED LIARS, SO YOU PASSED THE AUDIT EASILY.
WE SUCCEED WHERE IT COUNTS !!!

ALICE IS SITTING IN FOR THE BOSS!
S. Adams

PRODUCTIVITY AT LAST!!!
EFFICIENCY! YES!!
9/28 © 1995 United Feature Syndicate, Inc.(NYC)

AS LONG AS SHE DOESN'T GET AN ATTITUDE...

ALICE SITS IN FOR THE BOSS
I WILL APPROVE YOUR EXPENSE VOUCHER ON ONE CONDITION.
S. Adams

YOU MUST SLAY THE CREATURE WHO STALKS THE OFFICE AT NIGHT AND EATS OUR HIDDEN SNACKS!!!
9/29 © 1995 United Feature Syndicate, Inc.(NYC)

IT HAS TO BE EITHER YOU OR THE SECURITY GUARD.
SLAY HIM FIRST AND SEE IF THE PROBLEM STOPS.

YOU'RE MAKING A BIG MISTAKE. I'M NO ORDINARY MOUSE. IF YOU KISS ME I'LL TURN INTO A PRINCE!!!
S. Adams

DID I SAY "PRINCE"? I MEANT I'D BECOME THE SYMBOL FOR THE PERFORMER FORMERLY KNOWN AS PRINCE. HA HA HA!! GET IT?
9/30 © 1995 United Feature Syndicate, Inc.(NYC)

YOU'RE IMMUNE TO BOTH ROMANCE AND MIRTH. YOU MUST BE A... A...
THAT'S RIGHT. I'M AN ENGINEER.
TRASH

WISH ME LUCK, DOGBERT.
IF YOU GET MORE LUCK, WOULDN'T THERE BE LESS LUCK AVAILABLE FOR ME?
S. Adams

FOR "DESIRED SALARY" YOU WROTE "ONE MILLION DOLLARS."

YES, THANKS FOR ASKING.

PERHAPS THE QUESTION IS MISLEADING. THE APPLICATION SHOULD HAVE ASKED WHAT SALARY YOU EXPECT.

OH... WELL, I EXPECT YOU'LL HIRE SOMEBODY MORE QUALIFIED AND MY SALARY WILL REMAIN UNCHANGED.

10-1

NO, TOO HONEST. I'M LOOKING FOR SOMETHING CLOSE TO REALITY, WITH MAYBE TWENTY-PERCENT FANTASY LAYERED ON TOP.

OKAY... I'D LIKE A FIFTEEN-PERCENT RAISE AND A LITTLE SHOULDER MASSAGE.

WHY DOES IT SEEM THAT I'M THE ONLY HONEST GUY ON EARTH?
YOUR TYPE TENDS NOT TO REPRODUCE.

WE'RE POISED FOR SUCCESS. WE EXPECT HUGE EARNINGS AND INCREASED MARKET SHARE!
S. Adams

NEXT ON THE AGENDA... THERE WILL BE NO RAISES BECAUSE IT WILL BE A DIFFICULT YEAR...

CAROL, I THOUGHT I TOLD YOU TO PUT THE "UNITED WAY" UPDATE BETWEEN THOSE TWO AGENDA ITEMS.
OOPSIE.

YOUR RÉSUMÉ DOESN'T LIST ANY EXPERIENCE AS A JET PILOT, MISTER DOGBERT.
HOW HARD COULD IT BE?
S. Adams

YOU COULD SPEND A LOT OF MONEY ON SOME PRETTY BOY PILOT WITH EXPERIENCE, OR YOU CAN SAVE A FEW BUCKS AND HAVE ME DRIVE THE CORPORATE JET.

I AM UNDER A LOT OF BUDGET PRESSURE... AND I'M NOT ALLOWED ON THE JET MYSELF...
IT HAS A PILOT EJECT SEAT, RIGHT?

DOGBERT, CORPORATE JET PILOT
ATTENTION, PASSENGER.
S. Adams

I'M CAPTAIN DOGBERT. THIS IS MY FIRST FLIGHT. I'LL BET YOU WISH YOU HADN'T CUT THE CORPORATE TRAINING BUDGET.

FOR SAFETY, KEEP AN EYE OUT THE WINDOW... IF IT LOOKS LIKE WE'RE GONNA HIT THE GROUND, TRY JUMPING UP RIGHT BEFORE IMPACT.

DOGBERT, CORPORATE JET PILOT
THIS IS YOUR CAPTAIN SPEAKING...
S. Adams

IF YOU'D LIKE TO LAND SAFELY, THERE'S SOMETHING I'VE ALWAYS WANTED TO SEE A CEO DO.
10/5 © 1995 United Feature Syndicate, Inc.(NYC)

THIS IS SO NOT FUNNY.

THIS IS CAPTAIN DOGBERT WITH SOME GOOD NEWS AND SOME BAD NEWS.
S. Adams

THE GOOD NEWS IS THAT WE'LL BE HITTING TOWN TEN MINUTES AHEAD OF SCHEDULE...
10/6 © 1995 United Feature Syndicate, Inc.(NYC)

THE BAD NEWS IS WE'LL BE HITTING TOWN.

IT LOOKS LIKE THE PLANE'S GOING DOWN AND THERE'S ONLY ONE PARACHUTE.
S. Adams

GIVE IT TO ME!!! I'M A CEO WITH A HARVARD MBA. YOU'RE A DOG!!
10/7 © 1995 United Feature Syndicate, Inc.(NYC)

THAT'S MY KNAPSACK.
OLD JOKE

THAT'S FOUR HOURS THAT I'D LIKE TO HAVE BACK.
WHO CALLED THAT MEETING ANYWAY?
S. Adams

I MUST HAVE LEFT MY CALENDAR IN THERE.

OOOH
?

I'VE DISCOVERED A PRIMITIVE DONUT-SCAVENGING MAN CLAD ONLY IN YELLOW STICKY NOTES!!

I WAS ONCE LIKE YOU, BEFORE THE GREAT RIF.
10-8
© 1995 United Feature Syndicate, Inc.(NYC)

BUT RATHER THAN LEAVE IN HUMILIATION I DECIDED TO STAY AND LIVE OFF THE LAND LIKE OUR PROUD ANCESTORS.

TO ENSURE A BOUNTIFUL HARVEST I DO MY DONUT DANCE TO THE GODS.

WHEN THAT DOESN'T WORK I DISTRIBUTE MEETING NOTICES.
YOU'RE THE ONE!!

WE'LL SUCCEED IF WE UNDERSTAND WHO OUR COMPETITORS REALLY ARE!

MY COMPETITION IS DILBERT AND ALICE, WITH WHOM I COMPETE FOR SALARY INCREASES AND RARE PROMOTION OPPORTUNITIES.

I MEANT OUR EXTERNAL COMPETITION.
TELL ME AGAIN WHAT WE MAKE.
NO RAISE FOR YOU, IDIOT BOY.

I'VE DECIDED TO GET MORE INVOLVED WITH YOUR PROJECT.
UH-OH.
UH-OH.

I'M JUST GOING TO ROLL UP MY SLEEVES AND PITCH IN.

DOES ANYBODY KNOW HOW TO WORK THESE BUTTONS?

OKAY, JUST SHOW ME HOW TO PROGRAM SO I CAN HELP OUT ON YOUR PROJECT.

YOU'RE GOING TO BUILD A "G.U.I." USING OBJECT-ORIENTED DEVELOPMENT TOOLS...
G.U.I. IS PRONOUNCED "GOOEY."

I USED MY GUN OBJECT TO BLAST THE BUG OBJECT IN THE HALL OBJECT!!
NOTICE HOW GOOEY IT IS.

OUR ORIGINAL PROJECT TIME LINE WAS TWELVE MONTHS... BUT SINCE YOU PITCHED IN TO HELP...
S. Adams

I DON'T HAVE AN EXACT END DATE, BUT IT'S ROUGHLY THE SAME TIME THAT THE SUN BECOMES A COLD DARK CHUNK OF COAL THE SIZE OF YOUR FOREHEAD.
10/12 © 1995 United Feature Syndicate, Inc.(NYC)

WE'LL NEED FLASH-LIGHTS.
AND SWEATERS. IT COULD GET NIPPY.

AS DIRECTOR OF HUMAN RESOURCES I HAVE DEVELOPED A POLICY FOR HANDLING THE EMPLOYEES WHO COMPLAIN.
S. Adams

IT'S A BIG HOLE. I'LL TRICK THE WHINERS INTO GETTING IN IT. AND THEN I'LL COVER THEM WITH SAND.
10/13 © 1995 United Feature Syndicate, Inc.(NYC)

I DON'T SEE HOW THIS COULD POSSIBLY WORK.
THERE'S A DETAILED EXPLANATION AT THE BOTTOM OF THE HOLE.

CATBERT THE H.R. DIRECTOR
MY JOB IS TOO STRESSFUL. CAN I SEE A COMPANY COUNSELOR?
S. Adams

I RE-ENGINEERED OUR COUNSELING PROCESS. NOW WE PUT YOU IN A BIG HOLE AND COVER YOU WITH SAND.
10/14 © 1995 United Feature Syndicate, Inc.(NYC)

IF THIS IS MY ONLY BENEFIT I'D BETTER GET A LOT OF SAND!
JUST KEEP YOUR MOUTH OPEN.

WHY DO YOU WANT TO BE OUR NEW "LONG RANGE PLANNER," MISTER DOGBERT?
S. Adams

BECAUSE "LONG RANGE" IS VERY FAR AWAY...

...THEREFORE IT WILL BE IMPOSSIBLE TO EVALUATE MY PERFORMANCE.

IF IT'S NOT TOO MUCH TO ASK, I'D LIKE TO BE ON FLEX-TIME SO YOU'LL NEVER KNOW IF I'M SUPPOSED TO BE AT WORK.

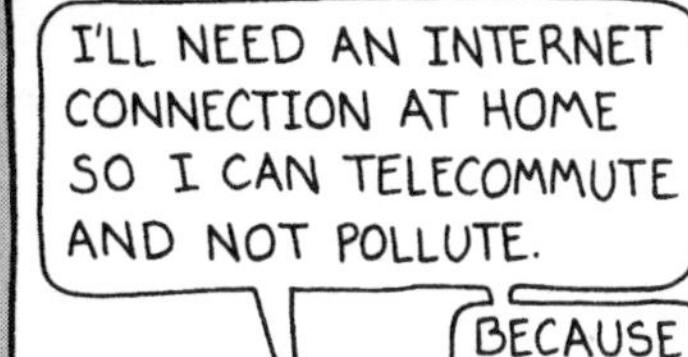
I'LL NEED AN INTERNET CONNECTION AT HOME SO I CAN TELECOMMUTE AND NOT POLLUTE.

BECAUSE I GIVE A HOOT.

10-15

ALSO, I'D LIKE TO BE IN A GROUP WITH LOTS OF LOSERS. THAT WAY I'LL GET THE BIGGEST RAISE WHEN WE'RE RANKED.

YOU'RE HIRED. ALL OF THE OTHER APPLICANTS DEMANDED RELOCATION EXPENSES AND I HAVE NO BUDGET FOR THAT.

WHY DO I HAVE TO WORK WHILE YOU JUST LOOK FOR POODLE GRAPHICS ON THE INTERNET?
DON'T WORK TOO HARD; I'D LIKE A BIG RAISE.

DOGBERT, YOUR MISSION IS TO TELL MY CO-WORKER THAT HER PERFUME IS KILLING US. WEAR THIS GAS MASK.

S.Adams

WELCOME TO HEAVEN, MISTER DOGBERT.
WOW, IT LOOKS LIKE YOU GUYS RELAXED YOUR STANDARDS!
S. Adams

DOGS ARE AUTOMATIC. NO MATTER WHAT YOU DO, THERE'S ALWAYS A PLACE IN HEAVEN FOR EVERY LITTLE DOG.
10/19 © 1995 United Feature Syndicate, Inc.(NYC)

I'D LIKE THAT BACK NOW, IF YOU DON'T MIND!!
WHAT KIND OF DISTANCE CAN YOU GET WITH THESE LITTLE "FRISBEES"?

MISTER DOGBERT, WE'VE DECIDED TO SEND YOU BACK TO EARTH AS AN ANGEL.
S. Adams

YOUR MISSION IS TO HELP PEOPLE IN NEED. WE HAVE GIVEN YOU SPECIAL POWERS.
WE'LL BE WATCHING.
10/20 © 1995 United Feature Syndicate, Inc.(NYC)

OKAY, SO WHAT'S THE PRICE FOR NEW HAIR PLUS BUNS OF STEEL?
AHEM
IT'S ALL ON THE PRICE SHEET.

ARE YOU SAYING THAT YOU'RE AN ANGEL NOW? AND YOU HAVE SPECIAL POWERS TO HELP PEOPLE.
S. Adams

EXACTLY. I INSTINCTIVELY KNOW WHAT PEOPLE WANT AND I CAN GIVE IT TO THEM WITH A SNAP OF THE PAW.
SNAP
10/21 © 1995 United Feature Syndicate, Inc.(NYC)

ARE YOU HAVING ANY TROUBLE CONTROLLING IT?
MY AIM STINKS.

THIS GRAPHIC SHOWS OUR BIGGEST OBSTACLE TO SUCCESS.
S. Adams

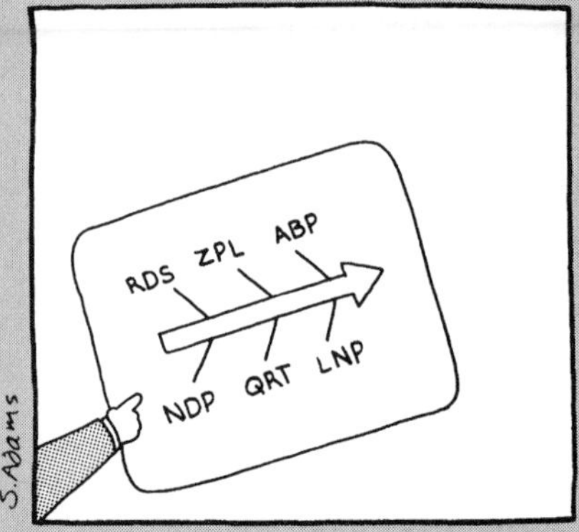
RDS
ZPL
ABP
NDP
QRT
LNP

?
?
?

ARE YOU SAYING OUR BIGGEST OBSTACLE TO SUCCESS IS POOR GRAPHICS?

I THINK HE'S SAYING OUR BIGGEST PROBLEM IS HIS OVERALL INABILITY TO COMMUNICATE.

10/22

I THINK HIS POINT GOES BEYOND COMMUNICATION. HE'S SHOWING US THAT HE DOESN'T EVEN THINK CLEARLY!
THAT'S IT!

HIGH FIVE!!
YOU BROKE THE CODE!

YOU KNOW HOW I SAID YOU SHOULD PARTICIPATE MORE IN MEETINGS?
I DIDN'T MEAN IT.

WE'VE DECIDED TO REVOKE YOUR ANGEL STATUS. YOU'RE GIVING US ALL A BAD NAME.
S. Adams

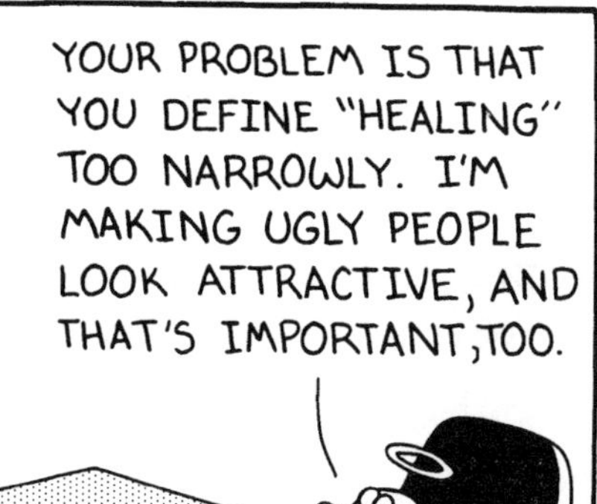
YOUR PROBLEM IS THAT YOU DEFINE "HEALING" TOO NARROWLY. I'M MAKING UGLY PEOPLE LOOK ATTRACTIVE, AND THAT'S IMPORTANT, TOO.

IS IT TOO LATE TO GO BACK TO MY OLD LOOK?
WHY? YOU'RE BEAUTIFUL!

CAROL, ABOUT THIS FLIGHT TO NEW YORK THAT YOU BOOKED FOR ME...
S. Adams

IS IT REALLY NECESSARY TO MAKE ALL THESE STOPOVERS IN THIRD-WORLD COUNTRIES THAT ARE EXPERIENCING REBEL INSURRECTIONS?

YOU'D BETTER WEAR THE INTERNATIONAL SYMBOL OF THE "RED CROSS" ON YOUR BACK.

TERRIBLE NEWS: MY BOSS ASSIGNED ME TO A FUN AND VALUABLE PROJECT.
S. Adams

UH-OH. THAT MEANS AT LEAST THREE MORONS WILL BE ASSIGNED TO SIMILAR PROJECTS. YOU MUST FIND THEM AND CRUSH THEM...
EXACTLY.

CARL, OLD BUDDY, WHATCHA WORKIN' ON THESE DAYS?
NOTHING FUN AND VALUABLE. SHOO SHOO!!

WALLY AND I HAVE A BET ABOUT WHY YOU ASSIGNED ME TO THE SAME TASK AS THREE OTHER PEOPLE.
S. Adams

I BELIEVE IT'S A CLEVER PLOY TO CREATE HEALTHY INTERNAL COMPETITION. WALLY THINKS YOU'RE JUST DUMBER THAN THE AVERAGE CAULIFLOWER.

MAY I POINT OUT THAT CAULIFLOWER IS THE BRAIN OF THE FRUIT KINGDOM.
YES!

THREE OTHER PEOPLE ASKED FOR THAT SAME INFORMATION. YOU MUST BE ON REDUNDANT PROJECTS.

S. Adams

HERE'S A BIG BINDER WHICH AT FIRST GLANCE SEEMS USEFUL, BUT YOU'LL REALIZE LATER IT'S NOT.

I'VE GOT A FEW MORE USELESS BINDERS. DO YOU WANT 'EM?

SURE. I'M USING THEM TO BUILD AN ADDITION TO MY CUBICLE.

IT LOOKS LIKE SOMEBODY IS USING BINDERS TO ILLEGALLY INCREASE THE SIZE OF HIS CUBICLE.
S. Adams

YOU THINK YOUR STATUS WILL INCREASE WITH YOUR CUBICLE SIZE, DON'T YOU! WELL, IT WON'T WORK!

HERE'S A RAISE. I DON'T KNOW WHY.
PSSST. IS HE SEEING ANYBODY?

HELEN, DO YOU HAVE ANY STAPLES IN THE SUPPLY CABINET?
S. Adams

NO, I ONLY STOCK THE BASICS: CHEAP PENS WITH GREEN INK, BIG JARS OF GLUE AND RIBBONS FOR OBSOLETE PRINTERS.

COULD YOU ORDER SOME STAPLES?
YOU NEED TO GIVE ME THE ORDER NUMBER.

OKAY. CAN I SEE YOUR SUPPLY CATALOG?
WALLY BORROWED IT.

I'D BETTER GET THAT; IT MIGHT BE PERSONAL.
RRRING
SOB

10/29

WALLY, DO YOU HAVE THE...
I NEED YOUR HELP WITH THIS. PULL UP A CHAIR.

I NEED BOTH OF YOU TO COME TALK TO A VENDOR THAT WE'LL NEVER USE.

THANKS TO TEAMWORK, I ALMOST STAPLED SOMETHING TODAY.
I'M SO PROUD TO KNOW YOU.

HEADQUARTERS
HEY, CHUCK'S LOOKING UNHAPPY TODAY. WHAT'S THE PROBLEM, BIG GUY?

ALL OF MY BAD DECISIONS ARE CATCHING UP TO ME. COULD WE DO ANOTHER REORG TO COVER MY TRACKS?
YEAH, I'VE GOT SOME BODIES TO BURY, TOO.
S. Adams

"...THESE CHANGES WILL ALLOW US TO FOCUS ON OUR CORE BUSINESS."
WHOA! LET ME GET MY REORG BOOTS.

I DON'T UNDERSTAND HOW THE NEW REORGAN- IZATION WILL HELP US "FOCUS ON OUR CORE BUSINESS."

DID OUR CORE BUSINESS CHANGE? OR ARE YOU SAYING THAT EVERY REORG PRIOR TO THIS WAS A MISDIRECTED FAILURE?
S. Adams

WALLY, WHEN A CAR GETS A FLAT TIRE, WHAT DO YOU DO?
WELL, IF I'M YOU, I ROTATE THE TIRES AND DRIVE HOME.

GUESS WHAT, WALLY.
WHAT SADISTIC PLOT HAS H.R. COME UP WITH NOW, CATBERT?

WE'RE GIVING YOU A REAL BOSS PLUS A "DOTTED LINE" TO ANOTHER BOSS WHO HAS DIFFERENT OBJECTIVES.
S. Adams

THE STATUS REPORTS ALONE WILL TAKE FORTY HOURS A WEEK.
I'M GONNA STAPLE MYSELF TO DEATH.

I HEARD YOU GOT ASSIGNED ON A "DOTTED LINE" TO OUR BOSS' ARCH-RIVAL.
GROAN
S. Adams

LOOK ON THE BRIGHT SIDE. THINK OF YOURSELF AS LEADING THE EXCITING LIFE OF A SECRET DOUBLE-AGENT!
11/2 © 1995 United Feature Syndicate, Inc.(NYC)

DON'T MOST DOUBLE-AGENTS GET CAPTURED AND EXECUTED IMMEDIATELY?
THEY WISH IT WAS IMMEDIATE.

THE "DOGBERT CORPORATE ART SOURCE" WILL PROVIDE LOW-COST PAINTINGS FOR YOUR WALLS.
S. Adams

OUR MOTTO IS "IF IT'S IN A FRAME IT WILL LOOK LIKE ART TO YOU."
11/3 © 1995 United Feature Syndicate, Inc.(NYC)

HOW MUCH DO THE PAINTINGS COST?
SIX DOLLARS A POUND.

HOW DID YOU GET THE CONTRACT TO SUPPLY OUR COMPANY WITH WALL ART?
LOW BID.
S. Adams

AS WE SPEAK, MY ASSISTANT IS SCOURING THE EARTH IN SEARCH OF LOW-COST ART.
11/4 © 1995 United Feature Syndicate, Inc.(NYC)

SCHOOL-o-ART
I'LL TAKE IT!!

I WORKED ALL NIGHT BUT I FINISHED THE PRESENTATION PACKAGE YOU WANTED.
S. Adams

PUT THE PRESENTATION DATE ON EACH PAGE.

THOSE ARE COLOR TRANSPARENCIES. IT WOULD TAKE HOURS AND COST HUNDREDS OF DOLLARS TO REPRINT THEM.

THERE'S NO REASON TO DATE THEM. IN FACT, IT WOULD LIMIT FUTURE USE AND CLUTTER THE PAGE.

BUT SINCE YOU'RE INCAPABLE OF ADMITTING ERROR...

11/5

I EAGERLY AWAIT YOUR BIZARRE, OTHER-WORLDLY EXPLANATION FOR PUTTING THE DATE ON EACH PAGE.

SOME PEOPLE MIGHT NOT HAVE CALENDARS. AND WE HAVE TO MAKE SURE IT'S NOT A HOLIDAY.
BAM!

OUCH. MY BRAIN EXPLODED.
THE FIRST PRESENTATION IS FEBRUARY 30TH...

I'VE COME TO BE YOUR PERSONAL DIGITAL ASSISTANT.
S. Adams

USE THE LITTLE PEN TO WRITE MESSAGES ON MY STOMACH. I'LL USE STATE-OF-THE-RAT TECHNOLOGY TO INTERPRET YOUR HANDWRITING.

WEAVE... ME... A... CONE... YOO... CUPID... BAT...

11/6

WHY ARE YOU PUTTING A SIGN ON THE COFFEE MAKER?
COFFEE MAKER
S. Adams

IT'S AN ISO 9000 REQUIREMENT. EVERYTHING MUST BE CLEARLY LABELED. THERE CAN BE NO EXCEPTIONS.
THAT'S STUPID.

BELIEVE ME, I DON'T LIKE IT ANY MORE THAN YOU DO.
STUPID LABEL GUY

11/7

THE PROJECT STATUS IS "YELLOW LIGHT."
S. Adams

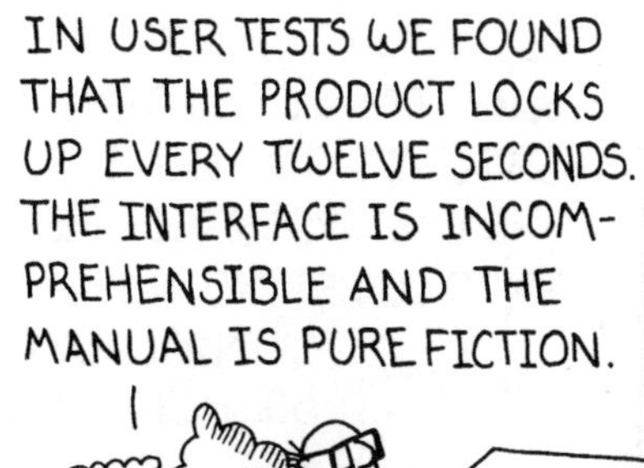

IN USER TESTS WE FOUND THAT THE PRODUCT LOCKS UP EVERY TWELVE SECONDS. THE INTERFACE IS INCOMPREHENSIBLE AND THE MANUAL IS PURE FICTION.

I THINK IT'S CLEAR WHAT WE NEED TO DO...
SHIP IT AND HOPE SOMEBODY WRITES A "DUMMIES" BOOK ABOUT IT?

11/8

SAINT DOGBERT ENTERS THE LAND OF CUBICLES SEARCHING FOR THE DEMONS OF STUPIDITY.

S. Adams

SUDDENLY HE FINDS AN OVER-PROMOTED COMPUTER GURU SPOUTING USELESS DATABASE CONCEPTS.

YOU'D BE FOOLS TO IGNORE THE BOOLEAN ANTI-BINARY LEAST-SQUARE APPROACH.

11/9

THE MONSTER IS DISPATCHED TO THE DARK WORLD BY THE SIGHT OF ITS MOST FEARED OBJECT.

HOW LONG WILL IT TAKE TO FIX ANY PROBLEMS WE FIND IN OUR BETA PRODUCT?

S. Adams

IT IS LOGICALLY IMPOSSIBLE TO SCHEDULE FOR THE UNKNOWN.

11/10

TRY TO THINK AS A MANAGER, NOT AS AN ENGINEER.

IN THAT CASE, WE'LL FIX THE PROBLEMS BEFORE WE FIND THEM.

THIS NEXT TRANSPARENCY IS AN INCOMPREHENSIBLE JUMBLE OF COMPLEXITY AND UNDEFINED ACRONYMS.

S. Adams

YOU MIGHT WONDER WHY I'M GOING TO SHOW IT TO YOU SINCE THE ONLY POSSIBLE RESULT IS TO LOWER YOUR OPINION OF MY COMMUNICATION SKILLS.

11/11

FRANKLY, IT'S BECAUSE I LIKE MAKING COMPLEX PICTURES MORE THAN I LIKE YOU.

MISTER CATBERT WILL EXPLAIN OUR NEW "TOTAL COMPENSATION PLAN" FOR EXCELLENCE.
S. Adams

WE NO LONGER VIEW COMPENSATION IN THE NARROW TERMS OF SALARY ALONE.

DANGER! DANGER!

IF EMPLOYEE BENEFITS GO UP, THEN SALARIES CAN GO DOWN AND IT ALL BALANCES OUT.

FOR EXAMPLE, DID YOU KNOW YOU COULD LOWER YOUR BLOOD PRESSURE BY RUBBING MY SOFT, FURRY BELLY?
© 1995 United Feature Syndicate, Inc.(NYC)
11/12

IT MIGHT BE A TRICK!
WHAT'S THE WORST THING THAT COULD HAPPEN?

HA HA HA!!! IT'S A HEALTH BENEFIT! NOW I'LL CUT EVERYBODY'S SALARY!

I'VE NOTICED THAT THE MORE HEALTH BENEFITS I GET, THE WORSE I FEEL.

OUR GOAL IS TO WRITE BUG-FREE SOFTWARE. I'LL PAY A TEN-DOLLAR BONUS FOR EVERY BUG YOU FIND AND FIX.

YAHOO!
WE'RE RICH
YES!!! YES!!! YES!!!
S. Adams

I HOPE THIS DRIVES THE RIGHT BEHAVIOR.
I'M GONNA WRITE ME A NEW MINIVAN THIS AFTERNOON!

THE COMPANY PAYS ME TEN DOLLARS FOR EVERY BUG I FIX IN MY CODE, RATBERT.

I WANT YOU TO DO YOUR LITTLE RAT DANCE ON MY KEYBOARD SO I'LL HAVE LOTS OF BUGS TO FIX.
S. Adams

HOW AM I DOING?
NOT SO GOOD. YOU JUST AUTHORED A WEB BROWSER.

MY ACCOMPLISHMENT THIS WEEK IS THAT I'VE BECOME AN AGENT OF CHANGE.

I FOSTER AND REWARD THOSE BEHAVIORS THAT CONTRIBUTE TO A CULTURE OF TEAMWORK.
S. Adams

I'VE BECOME SLIGHTLY MORE CYNICAL.
KEEP UP THE GOOD WORK, BUDDY.
PAT PAT

I USED TO WRITE PROGRAMS USING PUNCH CARDS... BUT I'D RATHER BE FISHING...

LOOK, YOU BEARDED ROAD APPLE, IF YOU ANSWER ONE MORE OF MY QUESTIONS WITH AN IRRELEVANT STORY I'LL SNAP YOU INTO NEXT WEEK!!
S. Adams

SOMETIME NEXT WEEK...
LOOKS LIKE A HOLE IN THE SPACE-TIME CONTINUUM.
DID YOU HEAR A SNAP?

I THINK WE SHOULD BUILD AN SQL DATABASE.
UH-OH

DOES HE UNDERSTAND WHAT HE SAID OR IS IT SOMETHING HE SAW IN A TRADE MAGAZINE AD?
S. Adams

WHAT COLOR DO YOU WANT THAT DATABASE?
I THINK MAUVE HAS THE MOST RAM.

FROM NOW ON I'M GOING TO BE MORE PROACTIVE.
S. Adams

YOU'RE FIRED!!

FOR WHAT??
I DON'T KNOW YET. THAT'S THE PROBLEM WITH BEING PROACTIVE.

WE NEED TO SHIP THE V-1 PRODUCT TOMORROW. I PROMISED OUR CEO HE CAN ANNOUNCE IT AT THE SHAREHOLDER MEETING.
S. Adams
THAT'S TWO MONTHS EARLY!!
WE HAVEN'T ADDED ANY FEATURES YET!!
WHAT WOULD WE SHIP? OUR LAB PROTOTYPE IS THE ONLY V-1 IN EXISTENCE!
NO...YOU WOULDN'T!
I'VE SCHEDULED PRESS TOURS SO YOU CAN DO DEMOS ALL NEXT WEEK.
ON WHAT?!
WE'LL NEED TWENTY THOUSAND DOLLARS TO BUILD ANOTHER PROTOTYPE!
© 1995 United Feature Syndicate, Inc.(NYC)
THAT REMINDS ME; I FROZE THE BUDGET FOR THE REST OF THE YEAR.
11/19
IF THERE'S ANYTHING YOU'D LIKE ME TO DO, DON'T HESITATE TO ASK.
YEAH, I'D LIKE YOU TO DO SOME-THING...
OOH... I THINK I SHOULD HAVE HESITATED TO ASK THAT.